the TALE of TWO COUNTRIES

B.K. Karkra has donned four different uniforms in his career: the olive-green of the Indian Army, the khaki of the Indian police, the grey of the National Security Guard and the black of an advocate. He has also written innumerable articles for leading newspapers and authored several books. His last book, *Rani Padmini: The Heroine of Chittor*, continues to be the go-to book on this subject and was consulted extensively by film-maker Sanjay Leela Bhansali for his magnum opus *Padmaavat* (2018).

He lives in New Delhi.

Also by the author:

Rani Padmini: The Heroine of Chittor

the TALE of TWO COUNTRIES

B. K. Karkra

RUPA

Published by
Rupa Publications India Pvt. Ltd 2018
7/16, Ansari Road, Daryaganj
New Delhi 110002

Sales centres:
Allahabad Bengaluru Chennai
Hyderabad Jaipur Kathmandu
Kolkata Mumbai

ISBN: 978-81-291-5150-6

First impression 2018

10 9 8 7 6 5 4 3 2 1

The moral right of the author has been asserted.

Printed by Parksons Graphics Pvt.Ltd., Mumbai

To the London-based 'Premi' family into which my dear daughter, Lily, is married

Contents

The Lure of Life Abroad

W ith stars in their eyes and hope in their hearts, Gursevak and his wife, Sukhi, landed at the Heathrow Airport of London. Balbir, their friend, was right there to receive them. Fortunately, the security situation then was quite well and England was not all that fussy in the matter of migrants either, so their immigration check did not pose any problem. They were not carrying dutiable items. They were, therefore, also able to pass through the Customs without any fuss. Once out, they found the cheerful face of Balbir in the crowd. He nearly flew into the arms of Guru and their hug lasted quite a while. When they disengaged, Balbir greeted Sukhi warmly. After the brief welcome, they busied themselves in recovering their luggage.

The couple's first impression of England was that somebody seemed to be in control of the situation here. The queues were quite orderly. Though the passengers did not line up all that straight—that was understandable for they were civilians and not soldiers—nobody displayed any inclination to break the queues. The traffic on the roads was heavy, but not chaotic. The city seemed to have maintained its simplicity and traditional grace. Clean and green London appeared magnificent, though there were no skyscrapers to be seen. People here kept mostly to themselves. Otherwise, however, they were helpful, warm and friendly, if you needed to contact them.

Heathrow was not very far from Southall, where Balbir lived. He had his small double-storey house nestled in a row of adjacent houses that together looked like half-a-kilometre-long barrack. Most of the immigrants from Punjab had settled in Southall and it was considered a sort of a ghetto. The settlers, however, had gradually converted this ghetto into a good liveable place. Almost everything that the Punjabis had a need for—gurdwaras, temples, mosques, malls, banks, restaurants, shops and offices—had come up here in the course of time. The place very much had some flavour of Punjab. It was a sort of home away from home for them.

Balbir had acquired this house on mortgage and lived here alone. So he had no difficulty in accommodating his newly arrived guests. He himself shifted to the guest room on the ground floor and handed over the entire first floor to Guru and Sukhi to live in complete privacy. He had arranged for their lunch from a Punjabi restaurant that day. By evening, Sukhi assumed charge of the kitchen, as if it were her own. It had been properly stocked in anticipation of their arrival. She cooked the first meal of rice and rajma (kidney beans) for dinner. Balbir relished the homely food that he had been missing for quite some time.

They then sat for hours in the drawing room talking about

their days in Lahore where they had spent some of the best time of their lives to begin with and later had to witness the horrors of Partition also. They particularly recalled their great escape from the city by the skin of their teeth. The couple did not forget to mention the assistance that Balbir had provided them in bringing them together, and Balbir got nostalgic about the village life in Punjab that they had left behind.

Finally, they switched over to discussing their plans for the future. The next day was marked for rest and settling down. The day after, Balbir was to take them to a manufacturing unit, engaged in baking of bread, buns, biscuits, cakes, pastry, etc. He had fixed up some work for them there.

'You must have heard about the ethos of the dignity of labour here,' explored Balbir.

Guru nodded, 'We are mentally prepared to take up any work to begin with.'

Besides, the facility of flexible hours of work was available here. They could thus choose their timings and also the hours of work they wanted to put in. Beyond certain hours, the benefit of overtime at enhanced rates could be claimed. It was thus decided that Sukhi would work for around six hours a day and Guru would stretch himself for as many hours as he could. This is what migrants did here to find their feet as quickly as possible. Simultaneously, of course, both of them would start looking for white-collar jobs.

Next morning, all of them left for the gurdwara for paying obeisance before starting their life anew. After that, they went to the place where Guru and Sukhi were to look for employment. The proprietor of the concern was an amiable Englishman. A number of Indians and persons of Indian origin were already working in his firm. He had found them generally sincere, attentive and hard-working, while the local fellows were inclined to mix fun with their work. So, he readily agreed to employ Guru and Sukhi after a brief interview and also assigned them their work. Guru was to work with a group that was involved in slicing of bread and Sukhi was to work in the packing section. Their working hours and wages were settled and they were told that they could join their duties the very next day. After fixing their employment, Balbir also resumed his official duties as his leave had expired.

Thus, all of them quickly got involved in a busy routine. Sukhi prepared breakfast and packed lunch for all and took care of other household work, besides attending to her job in the bakery. With her arrival, the general standard of tidiness and orderliness in the house had improved quite a few notches. Long-missed lassi and other Punjabi delicacies, like sarson ka saag, makki ki roti, karhi,* pakoras, etc. made their way in the home. Balbir felt quite good about this change.

As soon as the couple began working, they started sharing household expenses with Balbir and even persuaded him to accept some rent from them.

Balbir had initially protested, 'You are just like my family members. Don't ever think that you are overstaying your welcome as guests.'

---

*Sarson ka saag is a dish made with mustard leaves, spinach and some maize flour and served with generous amounts of ghee; makki ki roti is bread made from maize flour; karhi is curry made from diluted curd and refined gram flour.

They, however, eventually prevailed upon him to accept their offer.

'We also feel that we are but one family and we shall stay that way. Nonetheless, even within families, all members are supposed to share the earnings as well as the burden of work for the smooth running of the household.'

Balbir realized that if he did not agree to the sharing of the household expenses with them, it would hurt their sense of dignity and self-respect and make them leave earlier than they needed to. So, he reluctantly agreed to their sedate suggestion and the next few months passed pleasantly.

❧

Guru had brought some money along with him from India. Over the next seven to eight months, they were able to save a decent amount of money from their wages, overtime allowances and a bonus payment.

'I think that we now perhaps have the needed balance in our bank account for the initial payment. We could start exploring the possibility of buying a small house on mortgage,' Sukhi suggested to Guru.

'Yes. We could at least start working towards that,' Guru said in agreement.

They then threw a hint about it to Balbir, who felt a little sad at the prospect of them leaving his home. However, he was quick to realize that they had to eventually move to their own house. He, therefore, not only endorsed their idea but also offered to help them in looking for a suitable house and lending them money for the initial payment, if needed. They spent a few days in doing rounds of various real estate agencies and having a look at the properties offered by them. Finally, they decided on a small house in Southall itself. It was not in a great shape, but was within their budget. After the necessary formalities and payment, they got possession of the property. The house needed a lot of doing up, but they left it to be taken up when they had the money for it. After cleaning the place and tinkering a bit, they moved in after organizing a traditional ceremony, the Akhand Path, at the house to seek the blessings of the Almighty. It was a wonderful feeling to be living in a house in London that they owned.

By and by, they purchased some essential pieces of furniture to make their home more liveable. This process of furnishing continued for a long while. Guru and Sukhi had been trying for government jobs for some time. Eventually, both of them landed with clerical jobs in the grade of administrative assistant. They now had a steady source of income and felt settled. Until then they had been avoiding pregnancy, but now they thought it was time to have a child. They waited patiently for Sukhi to conceive, but for some reason it did not work. Possibly, the prolonged use of contraceptives had its adverse effect. Both of them had themselves medically examined for infertility. But they were diagnosed to be normal. IVF had not yet come into vogue and nor did it seem to be necessary in their case.

Months, and then years, rolled by, but they were still without a child. However, their faith in the Almighty and intense love for each other did not let despondency over childlessness overwhelm them. Not once a thought crossed their minds that the other partner was in any way responsible for this state. They did not take it as a godly curse either and stoically believed that if that was His will, let it be so. Periodically, however, they uncontrollably felt the stab on this count. Desire for a child, particularly for a son, was very much alive and so was the hope in their hearts. Still, there was no feeling of resigning to their fates on their minds, not yet at least.

Both of them had fixed working hours. They now had time on hand on weekends to have a proper look at life in London. They first made it a point to visit various landmarks of London which they had missed—the Tower of London, Prince Albert Museum, Natural History Museum, War Museum, Windsor Palace, Buckingham Palace, London Dungeon, British Library, Hyde Park, Big Ben, Greenwich and so on. They also started interacting with the settlers, especially the migrants from Punjab, more actively. In fact, they picked up some friends from among the whites also. Guru had developed a liking for alcohol. Sukhi, unlike what the other wives usually did, did not exhibit the 'holier than thou' attitude in this matter. It was not in her nature to act like a 'kill joy'. In fact, she did not mind giving company to her husband on occasions, sipping delicately from a glass with a small peg of gin inside. This drink in her hands lasted till the very end of the party. Their passion for partying and interest in cultural functions also revived.

They were fond of flowers and greenery. The space in their front yard was very small; it could just accommodate a few flower pots. However, the space in their backyard was sizeable for them to cater for three to four low-growing fruit trees, some flowering bushes and plants and even for growing some vegetables. They visited the kitchen gardens of various homes and also some nurseries to learn what could be grown in the soil and climatic conditions of the place. They then decided to have a grassy patch in the middle, surrounded by some small trees and bushes. A patch was also earmarked for some flowering plants and growing some vegetables.

Farming was in their blood, but they had yet to learn a lot about what could to be grown here and how. They, however, did have the aptitude and will to acquire the necessary knowledge. By trial and error, they soon picked up the necessary expertise and went with their hobby in all seriousness. The backyard was dug up to remove foliage and painstakingly prepared to plant seeds. Soon, the green shoots started showing.

'Look! Two tiny tomatoes are there on one of our plants. Soon there would be bunches of these hanging on all,' one would excitedly tell the other. They would then rush out to have a long hopeful look.

'And there! A flower is trying to peep out of that bulb,' Guru would point out to Sukhi with the excitement of a child being taken to the Disneyland.

'Yes, by tomorrow or day after, it would be in full bloom,' Sukhi would respond animatedly.

They tended their little garden with great care and fondness. Often they had to uproot the plants which were not doing well and replant them with added care. In the course of time they had a lush green backyard that yielded fruits, flowers and some vegetables.

Their success gave them some ideas.

'Sukhi, are you really happy with the sort of life we have

here?' asked a contemplative Guru.

'I know, dear, what you are arriving at. We are comfortably settled here, indeed, with secure jobs in hand, roof on our heads and a hobby to pursue. In fact, with you around, I shall always feel comfortable in whatever situation we are. But I can read what is churning in your mind. You feel that this way we will end up living an ordinary life, as our scope for rising in government service is strictly limited. Why not go for something where the opportunity for rising is boundless?'

'Exactly, dear. It is perhaps time to take another calculated risk. Why not acquire a piece of agricultural land in a rural area a little away from the city and set up a nursery there?'

Sukhi concurred as usual. In fact, she also did not like the idea of living under a glass ceiling. She also wanted to soar into the skies. Some immigrants from India had made their presence felt in various fields here—commerce, industry, education and even politics. She always felt why they could not try their hand at something out of the ordinary. Finally, they decided that Sukhi would continue on her government job for the time being and Guru would resign as soon as their project got going. They started doing rounds of the rural belt around London on weekends to look for a suitable piece of agricultural land within their budget to set up the nursery.

Rural England was a sight to behold. The villages appeared to be just chunks of cities lifted and studded there. These had almost all the facilities parallel to the urban areas—nice roads, electricity, running water, schools, small hospitals, markets and same level of cleanliness. Rather, these mostly semi-hilly areas looked better kempt and manicured. Here, you did not see dunghills or walls pasted with dung cakes or homes discharging their muck in the streets or cows coming home raising dust in the evening—the phenomenon described as Godhuli in India. It was a pleasant experience to be amid such scenic surroundings. This ambience of rural hinterland could do wonders to one's mood.

Ultimately, they were able to locate a moderate-sized piece of suitable land to start the venture in their mind. It was an undulating and idyllic farmland, with a small seasonal waterbody in it. Soon the loans for the purpose were fixed up by pledging the farmland they were acquiring, besides the personal guaranties. Balbir also helped in the matter by providing some loan himself and by standing as a guarantor. The fact that they were in government jobs and living in a house of their own, which had been partly paid for, also helped in raising the loan. They were thus ready to take the plunge. For a while, they felt that they had put far too many eggs in one basket. But that made them all the more committed and determined to come good.

They eventually had the farmland transferred in their names and got it fenced to secure their possession. They then secured electricity and water connections also. A small hut was built in a corner to keep the implements, fertilizers, chemicals and seeds. Ever since they had set up the small garden in their backyard, they had been rummaging through books to learn what flowers, fruits and vegetables could be grown in the local soil and climatic conditions. They also regularly visited some nurseries to have the practical know-how. Roses were the most difficult to grow. They needed lot of tending and expertise, but roses, as well as the plants, were in great demand. Sunflowers were the easiest to grow. Then, there were quite a few bulbous plants, like alliums, amaryllis, anemone, crocus, cyclamen, hyacinth, iris and tulips, that were also in fair demand. A few patches in the farm were promptly planted and green shoots started showing there. Their attention was then turned towards the marketing of their farm produce—flowers and plants to begin with. For this, they got in touch with various shops, big and small, dealing in flowers and plants. It was now time to pay their whole attention to the farm. Guru, therefore, resigned from his government job and started working on the farm. It was to be prepared patch by patch; some portions required terracing. Sukhi would join him after the office hours. On weekends and holidays, she was there with him from dawn to dusk. Soon, their labour began showing results and in no time some flower bulbs were ready for sale. Once the nursery assumed some shape, Guru and Sukhi started inviting friends for picnics to bring their attention to their project. The small money that their flowers and pots brought, gave them great joy.

Once the flowers and floral plants started yielding some worthwhile income, they started growing fruits and vegetables as well. In around two years' time, their farm was a flourishing concern. Sukhi could now afford to leave her government job and join her toiling husband full-time. After some more time, they were in a position to employ a few people from amongst the immigrant community from Punjab looking for jobs. They now also started thinking in terms of acquiring some more land adjacent to their farm or close to it and building another hut where they could relax and cook. From then onwards, there was no stopping them. Now, they felt their life together was on course; they were in full control of their situation and could look forward to making a fortune in their chosen area. They could be reasonably sure that the movement forward would be on accelerated speed.

A Motherland Left Behind

Whenever troupes with Jagjit Singh, Pankaj Udhas, Daler Mehndi and others came to London to perform, many from amongst the Indian diaspora made it a point to be among the audience. Sometimes, people would bring alcohol inside the venues; the performances, with the alcohol also playing its part, touched some sensitive chord in the Indian hearts and left them brooding and longing for the motherland left behind. Festivity, thus, got mixed up with sentimentality and some sadness too. It took the people's mind thousands of miles away to their homes, hearths, farms, friends, fruits, flora, fauna, lassi and sweets and all the other things they missed here.

Almost all Indian delicacies were available in London in the shops set up by the migrants. Yet, the sweets and snacks in the local markets tasted different from those in India and the proper Indian flavour was missing. Even the fruits and vegetables available here did not have the taste that they were used to back in their homes in India. But these were momentary emotions. Hardly anyone actually wanted to go back to the countries of their origin from London. There were far too many positives here. The racial discrimination also did not raise its ugly head all that often. The migrants generally lived here in peace. Most of them were happy to be here, even though, in some way, deep down, they carried the feeling of being culturally different. The settlers, particularly the generations of those born here, felt very much committed to be true to their salt. Still, the longing for the land of their ancestors pervaded their hearts all the time.

Back home in India, things were not all that rosy. The country still suffered the after-effects of hundreds of years of slavery. A large number of the wrong sort of people had managed to come to the fore in politics. The Indian bureaucracy, too, continued to be corrupt and inefficient for that reason. The ethos of democracy had not yet homed in their heads. They were designated as public servants on paper alright. But, in reality, they considered themselves as part of the ruling class and the people as their subjects. The police was badly politicized. It was not easy to do honest business here. Besides, India then suffered from the pangs of 'permit-quota-raj' and there were shortages all around. The only saving grace in the situation was that the Indians were blessed with high IQ and had the potential to do well where the atmosphere was right for growth. The nation's talents were thus always on the lookout for opportunities abroad. Even ordinary people saw countries like the US, the UK and Canada as gold-rush lands.

Certainly, England was a better organized society and the people here enjoyed a much better quality of life. It was also true that after being the rulers of nearly half the world,

England was now keen to be a multicultural society. In fact, the British were still scattered all over the world, mostly as rulers. They were present in North America, South America, Africa, Australia, New Zealand and even in Antarctica. Asia was the only continent which they could not hold on to. It was too enlightened a place for any aliens to dominate its mind. Asia has, in fact, been a sort of spiritual lighthouse of the world—after all, most of the major religions of the world originated from Asia.

Yet, the original rulers who had tasted blood in the world were not finding it easy to accept its former subjects as their equals. The situation was akin to that in India where all were constitutionally equal, but some were more equal than others for practical purposes. This made the Indian expatriates look eastward. They ate well, clothed well, breathed well and were housed well here, but more of a man lives in his mind than his body. There was something amiss at the mental level. England needed to do something in this area to ensure that all its citizens felt comfortable here. Otherwise, all expatriates were extra keen to prove that they were true to their salt and, if an occasion arose, they would give their all for the country that they had made their home.

Their situation was like that of a bride who had left her parental home for the matrimonial one, but was unable to forget what and those she had left behind. It was for her in-laws to make her feel at ease in her new habitat. When they failed to do it, the bride felt drawn to where and among whom she had come from. Even, otherwise, nobody can be expected to break with his past completely—life, after all, flows in a continuous stream. Thus, turmoil and churning was to remain present in the British society, till its borders were open for the people from outside and till the settlers settled down here emotionally.

If England was to follow an open-door policy towards its erstwhile colonies, it had to have a large enough heart. Perhaps, this did not happen to the desired degree. Thus, whenever there was a cricket match between England and India, the persons of Indian origin found themselves clapping for India. They somehow felt that their pride lay in the Indians doing well. The British boys, on their part, would indulge in loud whispers, 'I smell curries,' whenever they found an Indian amongst them. Otherwise, many of the English loved hot Indian curries and spicy preparations. They would eat samosas, pakoras and gulp golgappas with great relish, though their eyes and noses went watery while they were at it. However, the following generations of expatriates were beginning to stop looking over their shoulders, and were getting increasingly assimilated in the English ethos. They looked forward to their future here more than their past in India. And yet, nobody can forget about his roots altogether. Thus, some of the nostalgia for the land of their ancestors subsisted and kept coming back to them again and again.

During the British Raj in India, the rulers generally displayed the attitude of Romans in Palestine during the time of Jesus. They did not like to interfere too much in the Indian way of life. They did not treat the natives as proper human beings, either. They thought that the natives were caught in some sort of a time warp and it was the 'white man's burden' to pull them up towards a proper quality of life. In return, they expected them to look at the Englishmen as their patrons. Lord Macaulay, the learned Law Member of the Governor General in Council, boasted that the entire literature of India and Arabia was not worth even a shelf of a good European library. It completely went out of his mind that India was credited with the first book of the world—Rig Veda—which still existed and was held in high regard, while Arabia had triggered the first wave of Renaissance in Europe.

The British did not resort to wanton cruelty in India. Their democracy back home played a part to ensure that their colonial rulers did not deviate too much from the basic sense of humanism. Still, they could, at times, act as cool and clinical assassins when their interests were threatened in the colonies. What they did after crushing the patriotic upsurge in India during 1857–58 should prove this point. The First of August of 1857 happened to be the holy day of Bakr Eid. Frederic Cooper, then the deputy commissioner of Amritsar, celebrated it in style by slaughtering a demobilized unit of the native infantry. Anyone seen moving after the collapse of the rebellion was hanged by the nearest tree. These wounds kept aching in the Indian breast for quite some time. But, by the time the British decided to leave the country in good grace in 1947, the hurt was mostly healed. They left the Indian shores almost as friends. Anyway, the settlers here had completely forgotten what had happened a hundred years back. No signs of that bitterness and those wounds were evident anywhere. The only lingering feeling, still lodged in their hearts, was that India was the place where they had all the inherent rights.

The United Kingdom, being a vibrant democracy, provided

opportunities for the migrants to rise to high political stations. In any case, all the British citizens, irrespective of colour and creed, enjoyed the right to vote and this vote mattered crucially in certain pockets. There was some sprinkling of Asians in their House of Commons, House of Lords and some persons of the Indian origin occasionally held ministerships and mayoral appointments too. However, they generally did not get much opportunity to hold the ranks of colonels, brigadiers and generals in the British Army or occupy other high positions of respect and responsibility in the bureaucracy. However, the general quality of life was good for the settlers, if they could bring themselves round to living under a glass ceiling over their heads.

With the passage of years, the United Kingdom, in its wisdom, had decided to be somewhat selective about the Asians seeking permanent residency in their country. It was, thus, becoming increasingly difficult for Indians and others to enter England to settle. Those who had already found a foothold here, considered themselves privileged.

Life in Their Hinterland

✣

Gursevak came from a small village in Punjab, nestled in the greenery and freshness of farms. His village folks lived a hardy life, close to nature. By and large, they were happy and contented people. Radiance of health reflected both on their faces and in the size and sturdiness of their frames. Yet, they occasionally found themselves to be living on the edge. The freakish pranks of nature often disturbed them a great deal. Their prosperity and welfare depended heavily on the crops they were able to raise. Sometimes, however, the bountiful crops of commodities like onions, potatoes, cotton and sugarcane, etc. became, instead, a cause of misery to them because of the sudden crash in their price as a result of the overflow of supplies in the market. Their fields had the advantage of an assured supply of some canal water. However, this never proved to be adequate. Often, there were serious quarrels over the distribution of this water. Thus, the sight of monsoon clouds generally gladdened their hearts, while the untimely rains and stormy winds also brought a prayer on their lips.

Their prosperity and social status largely depended on the crops they raised. It was generally thought that the children of the households that had grain in abundance were deemed wise, even if they were actually madcaps—'*Jeedhe ghar daney oh dey kamley bhi sayaney*.'

Gursevak's family was of moderate means and lived in a semi-pukka house. This house, as well as a few others in the village, had the appearance of a fortress because of their massive entrances. These dwellings had to be fairly commodious because the inmates included a good number of animals—bullocks, buffaloes, goats and, sometimes, a camel too. The more affluent maintained an odd horse and a few dogs also. The entrance gates had to be high enough for the camels to pass through. Still, some things like the carts, ploughs, firewood and cow-dung cakes, etc. had to be generally kept outside. Some houses had a khund (wooden log) placed outside to serve as a bench for gossip with the friendly folks. Quite a few discussions over the matters of immediate concern in the neighbourhood were also held sitting on these.

After every crop, it was time to prepare the fields for the next one. The fields were first lightly watered for easy ploughing. Manual ploughing, however, was not an easy affair. Though the plough was pulled by the bullocks, one had to keep the ploughshare pressed hard into the soil to create deep furrows—there was, in fact, a saying in Punjab, '*Dubb ke wah, rujj ke kha*' (plough the field deep, so as to raise a good crop for your satisfactory sustenance). Moreover, it had to be kept in alignment, so that it did not jerk away from the side furrow. After the ploughing work, the roots and roughage from the last crop were painstakingly removed and burnt, leaving the surroundings engulfed in smoke. However, as the country was not that crowded then, atmospheric pollution was not viewed with any sort of alarm. After this, it was time for sprinkling of the khaad (bio-fertilizers) collected from the village roorhi (dunghill). The fields were then ploughed again and seeds spread in the furrows carefully. A fatta (heavy plank) was moved over these to ensure that the seeds got buried safely a few inches below the surface. After some watering, the seeds started sprouting above the surface and green shoots started showing. Thus, with every passing day, the brownish surface began turning greener and greener to the delight of the farmers. The farms, from then onwards, had to be tended with great care, just like we do for newborn babies.

Young wives and, in their absence, the other female folks of the household brought midday meals for the toiling males. These meals generally consisted of a good number of missi rotis, some cooked vegetable, the most favourite being the seasonal sarson ka saag or karhi. A pot of fresh lassi was almost always there. In the early phase of marriage, the brides also often brought pudding in some form, usually rice or grated carrots cooked in milk that went by the names of kheer and gajrella. Later in life, they had to be mostly content with a piece of gur—that is what life was like.

As the mealtime approached, the young husbands often looked homeward for their companions to arrive with a long veil pulled over their faces and a matki (small earthen pot) of lassi deftly balanced on their heads. Over the pot was placed their meal wrapped in a thick cloth. As their damsels were sighted, they forgot all about the pangs of hunger and instead felt terribly hungry for something else. Finding a cozy nook was not easy at home with so many members of the joint family jostling for private space. When standing sugarcane or cotton crop or tall-growing charhi (green fodder for cattle) fields were available to provide them cover, the young couples lost no time in disappearing deep into their hideouts in their fields where an inviting bed of twigs, grass and foliage was laid for love. The eager fellows often went for sex headlong.

The way their ladies dressed helped in the matter. The women did not have to be disrobed as they wore nothing that had to be unbuttoned or unhooked. They did not often even have undergarments to be removed. Their loose blouse and skirt that was made out of quite a few yards of cloth with numerous plaits could absorb all sorts of body fluids without the stains showing too conspicuously. These robes had just to be lifted and let fall. Sex was, of course, a slightly more cumbersome affair when the ladies wore kurtis and salwars. The knots had to be undone and then done again after the act. If somebody eavesdropped on them at the wrong moment, the lovers were left short on time to everybody's embarrassment. Anyway, a good number of conceptions took place in the open fields, with the standing crop guarding the couples from the prying eyes. Sometimes, the whistling winds would permit them the pleasure of safely letting out the moans. Still, the lovers had to be careful. They could not be oblivious to the rustling sounds occasionally making way towards them from some direction to spoil their moments of shared sweetness. After all, doors were open on them from all the sides. The blue of the skies and some odd bird flying above, of course, always had the privilege of looking at them in amusement. But this they did not mind.

All this over, they would suddenly feel hungry and settle down to have their meals. There would hardly be any utensils to serve the food. At best there would be a chhanna (a deep round bowl of brass with its edges turned inward). It would be cleared of the cooked vegetable, cleaned and used for having shared sips of lassi after every morsel. The vegetable would be placed on top of the rotis that they held in their hands.

Gursevak vividly remembered being often taken to the fields in his early childhood, fondly perched on his father's shoulders, with his tiny legs dangling on his chest. As soon as his mother was sighted with the pot of lassi on her head, his father's attention got riveted on her. He then collected children from the nearby farms to give him company for a while. Some ripening plants of chana (gram) were plucked and these were put on fire by collecting some dry foliage. The grain contained in their shells got roasted almost instantaneously. The children sat in a circle around the fire to enjoy the half-ripe, half-baked grains called hollaan. This nutritious snack tasted as good as anything else in the world. Alternatively, the children were given gannas (pieces of sugarcanes) to split the outer covering apart and pluck and crush the inner part, bite by bite, with their teeth and suck the juice. Both these ploys kept the children busy and amused for quite some time and afforded the couple a precious opportunity to be alone for some time. As the children settled down to enjoy their snack and drink, they would disappear to their favourite spot deep in the maze of the tall standing crops. Gursevak did not then know why he was pampered and bribed that way. He was to learn later at the dawn of his youth as to what was what—the farms not only produced corn, cane, cotton and fodder, etc., these also produced babies. He himself was also possibly the product of these very fields. Man and nature coexisted here in a state of eternal need for each other. The fields needed manure, seed, watering and human hands to come alive. The living needed grain, fodder, other crops and also, of course, the tall standing plants to provide them private space for pleasure and procreation. The cycle of life thus went on and on all the time.

The couples could rarely afford to go for a much-longed-for siesta after the meals, because the fields demanded a lot of attention and also there was quite some work to be attended to back at homes by the ladies. So, the menfolk reluctantly returned to their work in the fields. If there was nothing else to be done, the weeds from around the plants needed to be regularly removed. Their ladies would leave for home, often with a pile of charhi (green fodder) over their heads. Back home, they had to feed the animals, scrape away their dung and get the evening meal ready.

Mornings were an equally busy affair and full of hectic activity for all. The buffalo needed to be milked and then taken to the tobha (village pond) for a wash. The milk fermented into dahi (curd) in a greasy matka (earthen pot) needed to be churned for butter. This was done with a length of rope coiled round a wooden madhani (churner). The ends of the rope had to be given energetic pulls right and left, alternatively, with both hands to make the blades churn the curd. A U-shaped cover was placed at the mouth of the matka to ensure that the liquid did not spray out too much, while the movement of the churner was also not obstructed. It involved quite a vigorous exercise by the ladies of the household.

After the butter floating on the surface was deftly removed, the churning lady would scrape all the butter sticking to the churner and the cover with her fingers. She would then put her hand in the matka and shake the liquid vigorously several times to recover some more fat out of it. When she finally finished, a lot of invigorating liquid was still left in the pot in the form of lassi. Some quantity of the fresh butter was consumed. The remainder was preserved for being heated up to recover the ghee (clarified butter) part of it. This lassi was the mainstay of the family and consumed with relish. Some of it was usually still left in the pot for distribution to others. If not the rivers of milk, at least the streams of lassi did flow in the rural Punjab then. Fresh air of the fields and lassi consumption by the folks were perhaps the primary factors behind their sturdiness and vigour.

Lassi was also used for washing hair as it contained some cleansing ingredients and the greasy element still left in it helped in removing the dryness of the scalp. However, the chhiddi's (tiny flakes) in the lassi had a tendency to stick on to the hair. These had to be removed by running a generous quantity of water through the locks.

After the lassi was thus disposed of, the matka was carefully cleaned and filled with fresh milk diluted with some water for slow-heating in a hara (casket-like earthen hearth in which cow-dung cakes are used as fuel). The milk heated in the hara acquired a peculiar tang, quite agreeable to the persons used to it. Some of this milk was used up during the day for drinking or preparation of kheer, etc. A good quantity of it was left in the matka for being fermented into curd for the next day. Care was taken to ensure that the milk was in a lukewarm state when a fermenting agent—usually, a small quantity of leftover curd—was added to it. It would not ferment, if it was too hot or cold. In fact, excessive heat and cold are the commonly known preservatives that would prevent the milk from solidifying into curd.

The villagers, including the womenfolk, went to the fields before dawn and after dusk for 'jungle pani', i.e. for relieving themselves. They thought that this also helped in fertilizing the fields. In the absence of proper drainage, the hygienic conditions in the village were often very poor. However, people did have considerable immunity that generally kept them out of harm's way. Minor ailments were taken care of by 'Dadima ke Nuskhey' (traditional treatments and herbal medicines prescribed by the elder females). For the more serious ones, the patients were taken to the village vaid (an ayurvedic practitioner). In case of acute illness or serious injury, the patients were rushed to the government hospital in the nearby town.

Sports activities in the village were limited to wrestling and kabbadi only. The main sources for entertainment for the village folk were Giddha (singing to the rhythmic tune of clapping) for the females and Bhangra (a bold and vigorous form of dancing to the noisy beats of drum and music) for the males. These were performed on festive and celebratory occasions. Rarely, some professional troupes also got invited to the village for giving song, dance and drama performances. Once, celebrities like Surinder Kaur, Prakash Kaur and a host of others were invited to perform in the village. The show was meant for the menfolk. Many of them, having spent their time in the rough and tumble of the village life, were truly ecstatic over the prospect of having a look at these singing beauties with golden voice. Many of them had come fully prepared to enjoy the function to the hilt, carrying with them a few drinks inside. They started coming into their own as the nice-looking ladies began performing. One middle-aged man pushed a ten rupee note in the hands of a male artist saying shyly, '*Jee, ek rupaia tusi rakh lo, baki beebian nu de do.*' (You keep one rupee to yourself and pass on the rest to the performing ladies.) This was just the beginning. As the effect caught on, a voice rose from the audience, '*Ranna taan asli eh hain na, sada taan hun tak kandhan naal hi wasta paiya hai.*' (They really are the proper sexy ladies, we, up till now, have been dealing with emotionless walls only.) These comments indicated that the village males carried many suppressed emotions inside and felt that they had been missing on something juicy in their monotonous lives. They truly had an inner urge to move towards fashion and sophistication like their urban counterparts, but their situation did not permit them to do so. It was this feeling that had made many of them sell their lands and bolt out from their villages for adventure on the foreign soils.

The other source of recreation for them was the periodic melas in the neighbouring towns which were otherwise primarily meant for business deals in domestic animals. Here, business was mixed quite well with pleasurable activities like shopping for the ladies, sweets and swings for the children and just loitering around and some participative activities like kabbadi and dangals (wrestling bouts) for the men. Sometimes, circus shows were also organized during these fairs. There was, thus, something of interest or amusement for everybody. Village folks eagerly looked forward to these happy gatherings and even those who had nothing to do with the sale and purchase of animals came to the place in hordes just for the fun of moving around among the milling crowds.

The cake among the fairs in Punjab, of course, went to the Baisakhi melas on the 13th of April every year. It was essentially an agrarian, thanksgiving festival to God for bestowing fecundity on the farms for raising sufficient harvest to ensure that His children did not have to sleep on empty stomachs. All sorts of amusement activities were organized on the occasion. Colourfully dressed people came in droves to celebrate the joyous occasion, leaving all their worries behind. The shops set up in temporary sheds and the hawkers did brisk business in bangles, cosmetics, toys, cloth, food items, amusement games, etc. Swings and rides took care of the recreation of all, especially the children. Lot of socializing among the villagers also took place during these gatherings, resulting, sometimes, in matrimonial alliances. The festival got an added lustre to it when the tenth Guru of the Sikhs, Gobind Singh, founded the Khalsa on the occasion in AD 1799 to give a militant hue to his movement for freedom and justice.

On the whole, however, the opportunities for entertainment in their lives being strictly limited, quite a few of the hardy farmers got habituated to regular drinking to deal with the monotony of their lives. Liquor flowed more copiously in the villages on festive occasions. An odd few villagers among them made a nuisance of themselves as noisy alcoholics and often got roughed up and, sometimes, even beaten up with shoes by their senior folks.

The main source of liquor was its private brewing in the homes on the sly. This worked out quite cheap. The British government earned huge revenues from the licensed breweries and vends and thus, illicit brewing was viewed very seriously, as it badly hurt their revenue interests. Understandably, the British were not here for the welfare of the natives. Their sole idea was to make money and repatriate it back home. Anybody coming in the way of this objective thus needed to be dealt with sternly. So, the police remained under constant pressure both from the government as well as the liquor vends to curb the local brewing of liquor. It was thus a common sight to see police parties descending on the villages and dragging away the illicit brewers to the police stations in handcuffs for being given bad time in their confines. Still, the practice of illicit brewing in the privacy of homes could never be stopped. People used to drinking were often not able to afford liquor from the authorized vends, while they could not hold themselves back from drinking either. So, the cat and mouse game between the police and the illicit brewers on this count went on endlessly.

Mankind, for some curious reason, has always been excessively obsessed with the virginity of their women. The virile people of Punjab particularly remain on short fuse on this issue. It is true that sex is a messier affair for a female—first, because her internal organs are involved in the act, secondly, the sexual secretions also stay deposited in her and thirdly, she also faces the risk of unwanted pregnancy. The general perception is that just one false step on her part, and she gets polluted in body, mind and soul for all time to come, while the man, who is often the initiator of the youthful urge, stays pure! Once the news about the illicit act gets in the public domain, the village panchayats sometimes try to squash the affair by ordering the couple to marry. If the boy and the parents of the couple do not cooperate in the matter for reasons of religion, caste, differences in social status and mutual antipathy between the families involved, the poor girls get into grave trouble. The lone answer to their acute ignominy in such situations is often the village well or rather even death does not wash their sin in people's memory.

Strangely, nobody seems to understand that the main sexual organ is the brain. Pollution, if any, occurs there. Brain, obviously, is common to both the boy and the girl. So, the sexual act without social approval should be a sin for both or neither. Rather, as Osho convincingly says, if sex is a sin, the biggest sinner is God Himself, for He is the one who has put this impulse with a purpose in all living beings. Virginity is, indeed, something that could be cherished—sex is not the baring of the bodies alone, but the entire being. However, why should the female alone be forced to bear all the burdens of chastity? In fact, the legal systems and societies are at odds with each other on this issue. In law, rape and adultery are offences for the males alone. Consensual fornication involving unmarried females past the age of consent is no offence, except in the Islamic world. However, the societies believe in heaping ignominy on the women alone for all the three acts. Such affairs often lead to lasting enmities and honour killings in rural Punjab. Gursevak's village also occasionally got soaked in tears and tragedies on this count.

❦

His father's shoulders were still sturdy enough to carry him, but Gursevak had now grown up enough and preferred to walk to the fields on his own feet. His two sisters were grown up and had been married off when he was barely five. After their marriage, it was not often that they were able to visit the village. Yet, whenever they were able to make it, it was celebration time in their household. Most of the time they remained surrounded by their sahelis (female friends), curious to know about their lives in the matrimonial homes. Little Guru (that is what Gursevak was then called) was showered with quite a bit of love and fondness by his sisters as well as their friends. He, however, liked to loaf around in the fields in the company of the village kids. They loved sitting under shady trees, munching or sipping at something or the other gathered from the farms or the trees around. Guru, sometimes, lent a helping hand to his father in the fields. But that was when he so willed. Otherwise, his father never forced him to do any chores. Not yet.

The village folk did have some vague idea about the value of education and had somehow come to believe that the educated lived life on a higher plane. They did aspire to get there, but were never sure whether their children would be able to make it for them. Schooling was, thus, now becoming something fashionable in the village. Every family at least tried its hand at the trick and liked their kids educated to some level. Most, of course, fell on the wayside. When some child crossed even the matriculation standard, there was a sort of flutter in the village community. This qualification, in its wake, brought the broadening of chests in the family, visions of white-collar jobs and better brides.

Guru's village had a middle-level school catering for education up to the eighth standard. When a new kid from a well-to-do family was brought to the school, laddoos were distributed among the children to celebrate the occasion. The ethos in the school thus turned cheerful for a while. This also happened when Guru was taken to the school for the first time in all fondness. The fresher found the whole thing quite goody-goody for a few days. After this, the reality started biting and the monotony of routine began taking its toll. Soon, he started missing the freedom to be able to do what he just liked.

Thus, the villagers viewed every morning on weekdays a stream of small kids on their reluctant flow to the school with their takhties (flat boards of smoothened wood) and bastas (school bags). Generally, the heads of the takhties were tied to the strap of the bastas and carried over the left shoulders with the two dangling on the back and the front. The takhties were supposed to be cleanly coated with gajani (a special type of fine and sticky lump of soil) for the children to write on these with pens of reed dipped in shiny black ink. They were also made to use slates to work their sums on. Use of paper for the purpose at this stage was discouraged.

The children were also expected to bring their own hessian

sheets to sit on. The better equipped schools, however, did provide strips of coir or jute matting to sit on. The kids loathed the idea of having to sit on these for hours. They tried to cope with their dullness by constantly shifting uneasily on their seats, pinching at one another or doing other naughty things that often invited punishment from their teachers. As the bell rang for the day, they bolted out of the classrooms in jubilation like the prisoners released from the Bastille.

The teachers freely followed the policy of 'Spare the rod, spoil the child' in all earnestness. Thus, if their wards failed to rattle out what was taught to them or were unable to solve the sums given to them or did something naughty in the class, they often got unceremoniously slapped or whipped by the exasperated teachers. The most common punishment was to make the kids assume the murga (chicken) position—by squatting on the ground, with their arms passing through the legs from behind and the fingers holding their ears. The posture caused some discomfort and humiliation. When they displayed a tendency to sag to relax a bit, they got a stern warning to remain raised from behind. Sometimes, they were also ordered to leap like frogs in this position. The harder cases even had their raised buttocks caned to drive home some discipline into them. The teachers believed that such rough and ready methods were not only necessary to enforce discipline in the kids, but also to shove lessons down the unwilling throats.

Guru also had a taste of this medicine when he once failed to rattle some pahare (multiplication tables). The teacher asked him sternly why he was not paying attention to what he was taught.

He tried his hand on the excuse: 'Sir, there is nobody to help me at home.'

Giving him a hard slap, his teacher said, 'Perhaps, this will help you.'

The little fellow sat sulking for some time. But he was now determined not to have himself humiliated thus in the class. In the evening, he had a long session with his friend, Balbir, who was a brighter student. The next day, his teacher again demanded him to recite the pahare. Guru was well prepared this time and did a good job at the task.

The teacher called him to stand facing the class and put his hands kindly on his shoulders. Addressing the class, he said, 'See, how quickly he has learnt his lesson. I want you also to be good students like him.' Guru felt elated and his well-meaning teacher instantly rose to respect in his mind.

Many children left the school after the primary stage and some dropped even earlier or a little later. Quite a few, however, made it to the high school in the nearby town. Guru was one of them—to the great pride and pleasure of his parents.

British India: The Police State

The map of England has the look of a chicken. Napoleon once said that England would soon have its neck wrung like that of a chicken. But this chicken sat beyond the English Channel protected by its strong navy. Napoleon's hand could not stretch that far. This frustrated the designs of France against the island nation. In fact, Britain has not lost a war since the last millennium, except the War of American Independence, which happened to be a war against its own people. All this gave them a right to feel that they were the super people of the world during the eighteenth and nineteenth centuries when they ruled over nearly half the world and the sun never set on their empire.

If not super, they were certainly a smart and resurgent nation at that point of time. They were thus able to outsmart all European nations on their colonial adventure. Their achievements in the Indian subcontinent were particularly amazing. The resources at the disposal of the East India Company were strictly limited. In fact, it hardly had much financial muscle. It needed to buy so many things from this part of the world for being exported to Europe and hardly had anything to sell in lieu, except the cheap drill cloth fabricated on a large scale in the English factories. The proceeds from their imports were not adequate enough for their purchases here. They had to thus pay for the Indian and the Chinese goods in bullion. This was bleeding them white financially.

Intelligent as they were, they were able to read the Indian situation exceptionally well. It was then a weak and wealthy country asking to be won. Six generations of the illustrious Mughal rulers of the country (Babur, Humayun, Akbar, Jahangir, Shahjehan and Aurangzeb) were followed by weaklings like Bahadur Shah-I (Badshah-e-beparwah or carefree ruler), wasteful Jahandar Shah (he wasted a large chunk of the state revenues on his concubine Lal Kunwar), cowardly Farrukhsiyar (he was captured by the rebels from underneath a cot in his harem), inconsequential Shahjehan-II, licentious Muhammad Shah 'Rangeela', timid Shah Alam (he was in asylum with the Nawab of Awadh, having fled his capital out of fear of his own Wazir, or Prime Minister—the fear though was not unfounded, as he eventually got blinded by him on his return to the capital) and Bahadur Shah Zafar (who is better known as a poet than a ruler whose rule remained virtually confined to the Red Fort at Delhi). In the absence of effective central authority, the provinces had become autonomous. The Marathas lost the Third Battle of Panipat to Ahmed Shah Abdali unexpectedly, for no valid reasons. The Sikh power under Maharaja Ranjit Singh had yet to assert itself. Thus the country lay badly fragmented. On top of all this, there was no dearth of self-seeking elements willing to barter the country for personal gain. It was a tailor-made situation for the aliens to exploit.

A small army contingent of the East India Company was thus able to defeat the formidable or rather the bulky provincial army of Bengal at Plassey in AD 1757 with the help of a traitor from its own ranks. What gave the British the added confidence was that they could always withdraw to the safety of the sea in the event of a military defeat. This small battle unexpectedly became the first decisive step towards their sovereignty in the subcontinent. The next one, fought at Buxar in AD 1764, sealed the fate of the country. This was the battle against the Nawab of Awadh, with whom the Mughal emperor, Shah Alam, was in refuge. Being beholden to the Nawab, he reluctantly showed himself up in the battle by his side. Their defeat gave the British an opportunity to boast that they had defeated the Emperor of India.

The British, however, were not yet confident of claiming the sovereignty over India and were, for the time being, content to force the titular king to appoint the Company as the Diwan of Bengal. Bengal was then a large province, consisting of the present-day West Bengal, Bangladesh, Bihar and Odisha. This gave the Company an opportunity to squeeze maximum revenue from the landowners in the province through acute coercion, bordering on outright cruelty. Only a chunk of this revenue was deposited in the state treasury and sizeable portion of it was retained by the Company for its so-called service to the provincial government. The revenue surpluses thus generated were utilized to purchase opium from the Malwa region to export to China. The Chinese, in course of a few years, got habituated to the drug and came to be called the 'Nation of Opium-eaters'. When the Chinese authorities felt alarmed over this development and declared the opium trade as contraband, the Company started smuggling the drug. (This led to the two opium wars that culminated in crushing defeats of China. The Company was thus able to push a couple of humiliating treaties down the Chinese throat. These resulted in big commercial advantage to the East India Company.) The sizeable monies made from the revenue collections in Bengal and trade with China largely solved the problem of them having to pay for their purchases in the region in bullion.

Anyway, this part of it is history. We are concerned here with the lingering after-effects of the British rule in India. The country was eventually able to break free from their stranglehold in AD 1947, though sadly not in one piece. The idea of cheap policing that they had invented is still a cause of acute discomfort in the country. The British were able to grasp the Indian situation rather well. Being too few in number in the subcontinent, they knew that they could hold on to their windfallen colony through a policy of terror only. This awe had to be all-pervasive, so that nothing against their colonial interests brewed anywhere in the vast subcontinent. Until then, no authority at the central and even provincial level was able to exercise proper control on their rural hinterland. They thought that it was not worth the effort and the expense involved in it. Thus, the Indian villages went their own way without bothering to take notice of who governed their country or the province. Nobody really interfered in or tried to control their local governance. It was the British who showed the way in this area and held hundreds of thousands of the villages in the subcontinent in their iron grip without incurring much of expenditure.

For this, they needed a strong police force that would act as an Alsatian for the natives, in the matter of fear and a lapdog, in obedience to the British. Their problem was that they did not wish to spend much money for the purpose—they rather wanted to save every penny for repatriation back home. Their genius came to their help in the situation. So what they did not have money to spare for their policing need, they had political power in abundance. Some crumbs of this authority could be thrown to the natives and their obedience earned. After all, clout matters to man for the satisfaction that it gives and it could also be easily converted into privileges and perks, if not pelf itself.

The British, therefore, decided to try it out. The idea of having lovable 'London Bobbies' in their Indian colony was straight away discarded for being both expensive and unsuitable for the native conditions. In pursuance of this policy, they created the post of station house officer (thanedar) in the rank of sub-inspectors of police. They were paid a pittance in line with the salary of an ordinary clerk. However, they were loaded with such a colossal amount of raw authority as would be the envy of officers placed half a dozen levels above them. They could haul up any common man to the police station on the slightest suspicion of crime or any violent spirit against the British and play merry hell with his body and dignity. Generally, thickset and heavily moustached fellows, broadly answering to the description of Yamraj (the god of death) were appointed to the position. Besides taking care of the crime in their area, they were, more importantly, expected to be the hatchet men of the empire to deal with any rebellious ideas bubbling forth from under the surface. The British knew that the natives would never reconcile to their harsh and exploitative rule. They could never be won over, but could be kept suppressed.

On similar lines, some petty officials, like Numberdars and Chowkidars were appointed in the rural areas to act as the eyes and ears of the empire. They did not mind their paltry pay because they felt elated for just being on the side of the rulers. Both the station house officers (SHOs) and these rural functionaries were tightly controlled by the district collectors, mostly the British, and were hauled up, if they failed to safeguard the interests of the empire.

These petty officers in charge of the police stations, otherwise placed in Class III service category, thus came to wield tremendous raw authority over the local people. These officials with batons and bullets, more importantly with authority to use these, inspired awe and terror in the common people. Sadly, this system of cheap policing continued after the Independence. Subject 'Police' got assigned to the states in the Indian Constitution. Any political party coming to power in a state in the country began with hurriedly placing SHOs of its own choice in its police stations. The politicians resented the outdated police system only when they were at the wrong end of the police stick.

Gursevak also thought highly of the police officials out of the awe and authority they projected. They had the image of the knights in the shining armour who dished out hell to thieves, robbers and other unruly elements in the society. Gursevak himself wanted to be one after finishing his education. However, an incident in his village made him change his mind completely.

❦

That day, a Mazhabi (low caste) Sikh was brought in handcuffs to a rest house where the SHO of the area police station was camping on duty. The rest house was located along the national highway, passing close to Gursevak's village. He had been hauled up for suspected bootlegging. As usual, Gursevak and many kids of the village had followed him to the rest house to see the fun of him being thrashed. Many a time the police sentry on guard there had tried to send them away, but they would come back again and again as they did not wish to miss on their fun.

The exasperated sentry would ask them, '*Oeay tuseen soharao kee laina hai?*' (What are you little rogues up to?)

They would sheepishly reply, '*Jee asein padhake pained dekhane hain.*' (Sir, we want to see the accused thrashed.)

As the suspect was pushed before the SHO, he looked daggers at him for a while that made the man shiver. He then hurled choicest abuses and demanded to know from him why he did it and who all were involved in the offence.

The man meekly pleaded,'*Janab, mera Waheguru janada hai kee maine kuchh bhi naheen keeta. Thode bande aimen hee phad liaye hun.*' (Sir, my God knows that I have really done nothing wrong. Your staff has hauled me up for nothing.)

On this, the infuriated Thanedar barked, '*Aes saley dey*

dubb ke knonsade lao.' (Thrash the bastard well.)

Gursevak and other kids felt very amused when the luckless man was beaten up with shoes and caned mercilessly. When, at the end of this phase of his ordeal, he still pleaded innocence, the Thanedar was exasperated. But it was time for him to retire for his drink. He ordered the suspect to be locked up in the outhouse and settled to relax. The constables with him knew exactly what he wanted at that point in the evenings.

They hesitatingly asked, *'Aethe theka taan hai nahin. Kee kareey, Janab? Aah jehrhi jabat keetee hai, challu?'* (There is no liquor vend here. What do we do, sir? Would the seized stuff, i.e. the liquor seized from the accused, do?) The Thanedar was about to nod in acceptance when the Sarpanch and Numberdar appeared with a bottle of 'sangtare marka' (liquor with orange flavour, procured from an authorized vend). This brought a twinkle in the Thanedar's eye and they settled down to enjoy the drink. The constables were told to make merry on the seized stuff.

The trio of the Thanedar, Sarpanch and Numberdar first spoke to each other formally. However, as the alcohol started having its effect, they opened up:

'Kee haal hai pind da?' (How is the village doing?) The Thanedar patronizingly enquired.

The two had to say in flattery, *'Thode hunde sab theek hai, Janab. Thoda taan rooab hee aisa hai ke kise sale the majal hai key koey choon bi kare.'* (All is well here, sir, because of your clout. You are held in such awe that nobody can dare to indulge in any sort of mischief here.) The Thanedar was duly pleased to hear this and started twirling his moustache. Meanwhile, the inebriated constables asked him as to what was to be done to the accused.

'*Janab, lalten laga daiyeeh, saala bolda hee nahin.*' They were seeking his approval for tying a lighted lantern to his penis to singe his private parts. The Thanedar did not want to be disturbed in this state and dismissed them quickly by saying, '*Jo marji karo.*' (Do whatever you want.)

After a while, there was a commotion in the outhouse. The accused could not stand the torture and fell unconscious with a thud along with the dangling lantern. The kerosene got sprayed and it caught fire. The now-jittery constables were trying frantically to douse it. The startled Thanedar demanded to know what had happened.

He was told, '*Sab theek hai, Janab. Sala aimeen drama karda hai.*' (All is well, sir. The wretched fellow is pretending to have gone unconscious.) He did not bother to know anything further.

By this time it was dark. The liquor in the bottle had vanished into their bellies. The Sarpanch asked the Thanedar in formality, '*Janab, hoar magaeye?* (Shall we get more?)

The Thanedar said to their relief, '*Nahien. Hun khaana maga lo. Baaki kulh dekhan ge.*' (No. Let us have food now. Further, we would see tomorrow.)

They had their food clumsily, scattering bones all around them. A village sweeper was kept stand by to clean up the area. Before retiring for the night, the Thanedar went to have a look at the accused. He lay like a dead body in a corner.

'*Kuchh bolaya?*' (Did he open his mouth?) he enquired.

'*Nahin Janab. Sala chhattaya wa badmash hai.*' (No, sir. The wretched fellow is a hardened rogue.)

The Thanedar happened to notice two rats in the trap in the room. He ordered these to be put in his 'kachherhra' (underpants) to give him company in the night. The cord of his underpants was loosened and the mice let in. The cord was securely tightened again. His hands were already tied at the back. The agitated mice gave him a number of painful bites in the groin area and finally escaped after nibbling through the fabric, but not before giving a real agonizing time to him.

The Thanedar spent quite a few hours the next morning preparing the case report. Well before the lunchtime, the Sarpanch and Numberdar again put up an appearance with a bottle of liquor.

'Janab, bahut kumm karde hon,' (You work really hard, sir) they said in flattery.

'Baiyee, kee kariaye naukari hee aisee hai. Tusin baitho,' (What to do, brothers. My job is too demanding. You people settle down) he responded.

He, however, could not resist the temptation of the bottle for too long and said, 'Changa phir pao.' (Alright pour it in the glasses.)

After a while, his constables appeared before him with the miserable-looking accused.

'Janab, ehda kee karaiye?' (What shall we do with him?)

He ordered him to be hung upside down by a tree close to the highway.

By now some kids had again collected round the place to see the fun! The police people did not mind them as they appeared to be appreciative of the way they were dealing with the accused. The children seemed to look at them as heroes who had taken upon themselves the task of purging the society of rogues who understood the language of chhittar (shoes) only.

Soon, a motor car came to halt close to the rest house. A gentleman came out of it, followed by two decent-looking ladies. Indicating to them towards the toilet of the rest house he just walked away to stroll, so as to let the ladies refresh and relieve themselves in privacy. As they went towards the rest house, a dark figure hanging upside down like a lifeless object, with saliva from his mouth flowing to his beard, came in their view. The ghastly sight disturbed them. They went towards it out of curiosity. When they saw that the figure was a living human being, they wondered why he was hung there and by whom. They could notice a police constable standing nearby.

The older lady, with authority in her voice, demanded to know from the constable who had done it. The inebriated eyes of the Thanedar were following the ladies. The fellow went wild when he found the ladies interfering in the discharge of his duty or rather questioning his authority to do whatever he liked with his prisoner. He ordered his men to round up the women and produce them before him. Once before him, the ladies started arguing with him. The power-drunk and also the otherwise drunk man could not stand it. He barked in anger:

'*Machis naal salian the jhantaan phoonk do.*' (Show lighted matchstick to their pubic hair.)

His constables did have the horse sense that doing this to the decent-looking ladies could invite trouble. But they were secure on the fact that they were doing this under orders of their superior and the rare opportunity of having a look at the private parts of the sophisticated ladies was not all that unpleasant task either. So, one of them, taking courage in both hands, moved forward to untie the saree of the younger lady first. The elder one now realized what an ugly situation they were in and yelled at the top of her voice, 'SP Sahib.' Just the two letters were enough to sound an alert with the police party and stop them in their tracks.

The Thanedar was, however, still authoritative. Half out of curiosity and half out of apprehension, he asked, '*Oeh, tussien sohreo hoin kaun?*' (Who the hell are you?)

The SP who was strolling nearby heard the shout and rushed to the place. Not taking any chances with the local police fellows, he straight away introduced himself as a superintendent of police (SP) and also apprised them that the two ladies were the wife and daughter of the judge of the State High Court.

The kids were now due for a bigger fun that was to have a lasting effect on their psyches. The bewildered Thanedar did not know for a while what exactly to do. By now, the ladies were respectfully seated and the SP also occupied a chair behind a table. The Thanedar still could not muster enough courage to approach the ladies for an apology. However, he impulsively went under the table to hold the feet of the SP.

'*Bakash do, Janab Bahadur. Badi bhari galti ho gai hai,*' (Kindly pardon me, sir, I happened to make a terrible mistake) the Thanedar mumbled incoherently.

When he emerged from under the table with dishevelled turban, he appeared to be as miserable picture of man as the accused himself. The kids who had the image of thanedars as the knights in shining armour were shocked to see him in that state. The SP of the district was summoned post-haste to deal with the ugly situation. The SHO and the constables with him were straight away suspended and ordered to be 'Line Hazir', i.e. posted to the district police line till the completion of enquiry in the case.

Gursevak learnt something very funny that day—that the policemen were also, after all, human. He was to learn later that the policemen were very much human. However, the legacy that had come down to them from the British was inhuman.

They had to remain on duty and under stress all the time. The stress of having to deal with criminals of all hues, enquiries, legal action and public contempt that they faced was even more than the risk of dying in wars that the soldiers faced.

Then, it was also not a case of a rotten fish spoiling a tank, but a rotten inheritance spoiling the entire show. It was not a problem related to stray incidents, but of ingrained attitudes. The government servants in general and the policemen in particular, had yet to learn that though they were on the side of the rulers, but people were no longer their subjects, but masters. They were, in fact, the paid servants of the people. Anyway, Gursevak once dreamt of becoming a Thanedar himself. Now, he did not want to be one. Unfortunately, he had seen the wrong side of the coin. The police certainly had a shiny side too. After all, they produced the most precious wealth for the nation—the wealth of peace.

Urban Ethos

❧

Little Guru was now young Gursevak Singh Grewal, admitted to a government high school of a market town in the princely state of Kapurthala. He had quite a few students of his old school for company there for whom he continued to be 'Guru'. Most of them walked as a group for around two and a half kilometres daily to get to their new school. The very privilege of wielding pen and pencil over paper, rather than having to write on slates and takhties and just the exposure to the urban ethos made them feel good for some time.

The town was a small commercial as well as industrial hub of the area. Besides the high school, it had the kachehries (court complex), a hospital, a police station, a civil supply office, a railway station and many other-lower level government offices. It was essentially a gated town that was gradually pouring beyond its intended boundaries. In the absence of electricity, lighted gas lamps were hung on its gates as it started getting dark. This ensured some nocturnal activity in the early hours of the night in the immediate vicinity of the lighted gates and even some distance beyond. If nothing else, some groups of students would gather close to the gates to study. They would often go to the halwai (sweetmeat seller) shops to have a glass of thick milk with generous amounts of malai (cream) over it. The habitations outside, of course, went into complete hibernation as darkness started spreading its wings.

The town was a busy place throbbing with activity. Particularly, in the harvesting season one saw its roads cluttered with bullock and camel carts, discharging their farm produce in heaps by tilting their carts, not on the roads and chabutras (paved space in front of the shops) alone, but also on the streets close by. The heaps of grain, cotton and vegetables were then taken over by the arthiyas (auctioneers) and sold out in a few hours' time. The auctioneers collected their commission, and the farmers the rest of the price for their produce from the businessmen, usually having shops in the mandi. The generally illiterate farmers understood the accounts in twenties of rupees. Their typical conversation with the bania (shopkeeper) would go something like this: They would often ask, 'Seth Jee, kinna hogaya?' (How much am I to get, Seth Jee?) If the Seth said, 'Baiye, tere ek so ikkie rupaiye ban gaiye.' (₹121 are payable to you) 'Beehan kae hoiyian, aehey dasso,' (Tell me how many twenties I am to get) the confused man would ask. He would be told, 'Baiye, chhee bihan, te ek rupaiya upar di ho gaya.' (Your dues come to one rupee over the six twenties.) 'Changa, chhee bihan phadao aur ek rupaiye da gurh pa dayo.' (Give me six twenties and settle the rest with jaggery for one rupee.) This being the situation, the illiterate farmers often got fleeced at the hands of the wily businessmen. Nonetheless, those were the times when the sight of a hundred rupee note would send the pulse of a common man pounding. Thus, the one hundred and twenty rupee notes in hand would make the farmer feel for a while, in what way he was less than Birla, the billionaire?

To the great delight of Gursevak, the place had a cinema theatre also. Its hall being roofless, movies here could be screened at night only. However, before the darkness descended, the loudspeaker mounted high on the cinema wall started blurting, full blast, popular movie songs to attract the patrons. The tickets ranged from five aannas for a seat on the tarpaulin spread on the ground in front, ten aannas for the benched enclosure in the middle and one and quarter rupees for the rows of chairs placed at the back. The viewers on the ground in front had to strain their necks quite a bit to view the picture. The rows at the back were mostly occupied by the moneyed seths (rich businessmen) or the freeloaders, generally the influential government functionaries, their friends and families.

Gursevak was occasionally able to cook up some excuse to stay back for the night in the town to see a movie. He had reached a stage in his life when any good-looking woman would seem to be filled with sweetness. The sight of lovely vivacious women on the screen made him feel moonstruck. The memories of this gala time lingered in his mind for days together. How he wished that he could be in the cinema hall on a daily basis! He would not mind all the strain in his neck watching movies from the front enclosure. The theatre had a single projector. So there had to be a number of intervals for the change of reels. There was no electricity either, so the screening was managed with the help of a generator which broke down quite frequently and thus, the screen went blank and the hall would be engulfed in darkness to the great dismay and annoyance of the viewers. The more impatient among them would then start raising the shouts, '*Lait oey lait!*' (Lights, damn it, lights!)

The Mandi Afsar (a sort of city magistrate) was the most important functionary of the town. He was vested with quite some judicial as well as executive authority to manage public order at the place. Everybody appeared to be in awe of his official clout. The town was a politically active place. Political gatherings, rallies, agitations and processions were a common sight here. On such occasions, people often poured into the mandi from surrounding villages to create and complicate the law-and-order situations in the area. So, the Mandi Afsar would often issue prohibitory orders for outsiders not to enter the town. He would then go on his round of inspection, riding his official mare imperiously, with his orderly in tow. If any villager was located loitering in the town in violation of the prohibitory orders, he would have the punishment delivered to him on the spot—'*Maro saale ke char joote, aur bhagao isko.*' (Give him a few blows with a shoe and banish him from here.) The puny-looking orderly was always good enough to carry out the punishment to the six-footer sturdy jutts (Sikh farmers). After all, he had the mighty force of law behind him. The humiliated delinquent would then vanish from the spot in a humble hurry with his head bowed down.

This, however, would appear to be nothing before what his counterpart enacted some years back. He had Pandit Jawaharlal Nehru and his companion bundled off to the state capital, Nabha, in handcuffs to stand trial for violating his prohibitory orders at the place, about which the future prime minister of the country could not have known. When asked about the law under which they were arrested, the exasperated magistrate furiously retorted, 'Koi kanoon kanoon nahin. Hamara zuban hee kanoon hai.' (What law are you talking about? I am the law unto myself.) At Nabha, they were put in a kothari (cell) of a jail where mice were running all over and around them all the while, especially at nights. Ultimately, Motilal Nehru had to employ all his influence to have them somehow released after a fairly long incarceration. An Autobiography by Pandit Jawaharlal Nehru mentions about this clumsy incident.

The Mandi Afsar occupied a government bungalow as his official residence. It was a fairly gorgeous and imposing building by local standards and had the aura of a Raj Bhawan. (Governor's bungalow) about it. On every festive occasion, the local captains of commerce and industry (the seths) made a beeline to this place, carrying daallies (baskets of sweets and fruit) as a sort of tribute to him. His son, Keshav, studied along with Gursevak in his class. However, his being a student in this school was like Prince Harry serving in the British Army. Rather than studying, he was seen as gracing the institution. Everybody felt beholden if the elite fellow displayed even a faint gesture of interest or friendship towards him. Fortunately, he was not the unruly type and did not create any problems for the teaching staff.

Both Keshav and Gursevak were mediocre students. They were otherwise of a shy and respectful nature. These common traits brought them together and they were often seen sharing notes huddled together to the envy of many. The Mandi Afsar had arranged for a teacher to give tuitions to his son. The teacher was happy to do it gratis. Keshav ensured that Gursevak also sat by his side and was able to avail the teacher's help. Keshav also occasionally took Gursevak along to the cinema where he and the boys in his tow had a free access all the time.

Just a few trains passed at the small railway station of the town and in the evenings it emerged as a favourite socializing spot for the citizens. After having their meals in the evening they would gingerly walk towards the railway station, chewing paan or munching at crispy papad. They would then walk along the platforms in the manner of the people walking in a park and finally end up on the benches as the gossiping groups. Occasionally, some even dozed off there and had to be woken up by the accompanying friends. They would then let out, 'Thank you, yaar,' and proceed on their reluctant sleepwalk to their homes.

For the matriculation examination, English, Mathematics and General Knowledge were the compulsory subjects. Besides, one could choose two optional subjects from Hindi, Punjabi, Urdu, Sanskrit, Civics and Drawing. English and Mathematics carried 200 marks each and the three others subjects, 150 each, thus forming an aggregate of 850 marks. Pass percentage was 33 per cent of the total marks and it was necessary to pass in the English and Mathematics papers. This meant a minimum of 66 marks in each of the two papers. Besides, one could afford to fail in one of the other three subjects or may not even appear in that. Thus, 50 marks were required in each of the remaining two papers. So, the bare minimum marks for becoming a proud 'Matriculate' were just 232 out of 850, if one was able to cut too fine in all the four papers. There used to be quite a few examinees scraping through with round about the minimum score, indicating the generosity of the examiners in the marginal cases.

The bright Balbir, if you remember him, passed creditably with a first division score of over 60 per cent. Keshav and Gursevak qualified securing second division. One more student from Gursevak's village scraped through with 235 marks, while the others fell on the wayside, mostly to return to their farm life. Nonetheless, there was quite some jubilation in the village. After all, three of their triumphant sons had done the village proud. Now, the village could boast of half a dozen properly educated young men in its midst.

❦

Gursevak had an uncle, Gurbux Singh, settled in Lahore. He was a clean-shaven Sikh, employed in a British ordinance depot as a supervisor. He had his residence in a small two-roomed house in Basant Nagar, a suburb of the city. He was a moderately paid employee, but was able to earn sizeable extra amount through overtime in those days of World War II and thus the family could be said to be reasonably well off. What added to his clout in the colony was that he went to work on his bicycle!

Enthused with the presence of a well-placed brother at Lahore, Gursevak's father got him admitted to the D.A.V. College there in the First Arts (FA) class. Balbir also followed him there. After spending around a month with his uncle's family, Gursevak somehow began feeling uncomfortable and decided to stay independently.

The family was also not all that keen to keep him. Yet, his aunt asked in formality, 'Nahin, nahin puttar. Bahar ja ke kithe raho ge?' (No, son. Where are you going to stay after going from here?)

He did not have much difficulty in convincing her and his uncle that he would join his friend from the village, Balbir, who had been able to rent a room just a short distance away from their place. While living with him he would be able to concentrate on his studies better. He also promised that he would visit them quite often. After registering their show of reluctance and concern, they finally agreed to let him stay independently in the larger interest of his studies and wrote to his parents back in the village something like, 'Jee aseen taan bahut keha. Par kake ne padhai pichhey alag rahan waste aina jor paya key sanu akhir jhukna hi paiya.' (We tried hard to persuade him to stay on with us. But, he strongly insisted on living separately in the interest of his studies. We had to per force agree with him.)

Balbir had managed to hire a room at ₹5 per month in Basant Nagar itself. Being close to each other and both being on a shoestring budget, they were happy to live together. Besides the company considerations, they had the financial advantage of a single shared establishment. They had an electric light-point in the room, but they could not afford to have a fan. Even bicycles were then a luxury far beyond the means of the common people like them. They, nonetheless, had sturdy legs to carry themselves distances during their leisure to all parts of the sprawling city. As they were settling down, they had already managed several rounds of the gorgeous Gol Bagh, glittering Anarkali Bazar and the splendid Shalimar Bagh. These popular public spots were among the places that gave the magnificent metropolis its identity. Close to Anarkali Bazar, quiet flowed the river Ravi. Its western bank was often the venue of many fairs. It was particularly bustling with colourfully dressed people on the festival of Baisakhi and the kite fliers on the occasion of Basant Panchmi that signalled the end of winter.

The city had a magnificent museum and a sprawling zoo. Tickets to these places were very moderately priced. Balbir and Gursevak had already had a look at these. There were a number of cinema halls too in the city. Their lure certainly lingered inside their breasts on the quiet, but they had money barely enough to meet their essential needs and did not have a heart to ask their parents for more.

Lahore stands soaked in history. A legend has it that Lahore (Loh Kote of the ancient era) was founded millennia back by none other than Luv, one the twin sons of Rama who is considered to be the incarnation of Vishnu by the Hindu faithful. A temple dedicated to Luv was still there inside the Lahore fort. His dynasty ruled the kingdom till its last ruler, Kanak Sen, shifted to Ballabhipura in Gujarat sometime around AD 144. The city does not have any ancient temples because the early Aryans believed in worshipping in the open. The kingdom remained in Hindu hands till the end of the first millennium AD. In AD 1021, Sultan Mahmud of Ghazni destroyed it and placed it under the rule of his governor, Malik Ayaz. After a long stint of Muslim domination, Lahore became part of the dominions of Maharaja Ranjit Singh in the early years of the nineteenth century. Finally, it passed on to the British after the two Sikh wars of mid-nineteenth century. The city had got wrapped in a composite culture as a result of all these upheavals in its history.

When Gursevak and Balbir landed in the metropolis, something was simmering under the surface in Lahore. First, there was a surge to overthrow the alien rule in the subcontinent. The nation was in some sort of a mood for martyrdom and singing 'Maaye, mera rang de basanti chola' (Mother, dye my clothes in saffron for me to be ready for martyrdom) and 'Khainch key liee hai hum ko qatal hone ki umeed. Dekhna hai zor kitna bazuae qatil mein hae.' (It is the impulse to get killed that has brought us here. We would like to see, if the killer has strength enough to kill us.) The British seemed to be realizing that resurgent India had become too hot a potato to hold in their hands any longer. In fact, the jewel of their crown had already started slipping through their fingers. Wise and intelligent as they were, they had read the writing on the wall and were now preparing for homeward journey in good grace, leaving behind as little bitterness about their rule as possible.

Secondly, the smell of independence had fuelled some fears in the Muslim community. They largely constituted the landed aristocracy in Punjab, but had been rapidly losing their lands to the Hindu moneylenders. For some mysterious reasons, when they lived together with the better educated and thrifty Hindus, they tended to get driven to menial status in the society. Mohammed Ali Jinnah, a towering personality of the

Muslim League party, had seen this coming and did not relish the thought of his community getting reduced to becoming hewers of wood and drawers of water in the subcontinent. So, an idea was floated that Hindus and Muslims could just not gel together, as if they were genetically different, despite being the closest kin! This 'two-nation' theory had pumped lot of communal tension in Punjab and was gradually bringing the incipient bitterness between the two communities to the fore. One rabidly inclined Muslim wrote a communally explosive book, *Sita ka Sarha* (Rape of Sita). Not to be outdone in stupidity, a Hindu writer retaliated with *Rangeela Rasool*, and its publisher got fatally stabbed for it. A holocaust was clearly building on the horizon.

Lahore was thus in the midst of tumultuous times. Quite a few students from the colleges of the city were attracted to the freedom movement. In late 1945, the three former British Army officers—Captain P.K. Sehgal, Lieutenant G.S. Dillon and Captain Shah Nawaz—who, on capture and release by the Japanese, had joined the Indian National Army of Subhas Chandra Bose to fight instead for the independence of India, were court-martialled for treason at the Red Fort in Delhi. The air outside the Fort was rent with the slogan: '*Lal Qile se aaee awaz, Sehgal, Dillon, Shah Nawaz, Teenon ki ho umar daraaz*'. (There is a voice resounding from the historic Red Fort that Sehgal, Dillon and Shah Nawaz may all have a long life ahead.) They were duly convicted for waging war against the Crown and would have been routinely put to death. However, keeping the prevailing political situation in the country, they were spared the death sentence and were just ordered to be cashiered out of the Army. Upon release, they emerged as great freedom fighters of the nation.

A function was organized at Gol Bagh in Lahore to felicitate them. The British government did not relish the idea of their cashiered officers being publicly honoured. So, lot of trouble was anticipated at the venue. Despite that, Gursevak and Balbir decided to participate in the ceremony. They were fired by the fact that some years back, Bhagat Singh and his associates had haloed the precincts of their college while escaping through it after attempting to kill James Scott, the Superintendent of Police responsible for raining fatal lathi blows on the much respected Lala Lajpat Rai. They, of course, instead happened to kill Assistant Superintendent of Police, John Saunders, as a result of mistaken identity. Even the common people had thronged the place with their women and children and stuck on the spot defiantly, braving frequent baton charges by the police. The people went hoarse shouting, '*Lal Qile se huae azaad, Sehgal, Dillon, Shah Nawaz!*' (Hurrah! Sehgal, Dillon Shah Nawaz have in the end been released from the Red Fort) Since Gursevak and Balbir had positioned themselves close to the stage, they got quite a few baton blows on their bodies. Upon returning to their house, they tended each other with affectionate care. 'You have got quite a nasty blow on your shoulder, Guru. It is going to leave a scar on you,' whispered Balbir while pressing the spot softly with a warm pad of cloth to keep the swelling suppressed. 'I would love to wear this mark as a medal from our freedom struggle,' replied Guru with a surge of pride in his voice.

'Rather, I wish that I could do something more for the

country. But you have also got some serious injuries, Ballu. Let me help you.'

'I am absolutely fine. Do not worry. Good that we are also now part of our freedom movement, though, indeed, in a minor way,' said Balbir. Their feelings reflected the general mood in the country at the time.

Balbir and Gursevak were quite happy having their meals at the dhabas or sometimes cooking it at their own place. Sometimes, they also received canisters full of panjeeri (a sweet made out of wheat flour roasted in generous amount of ghee, with sugar mixed in it) from their homes. This nutritious stuff came handy whenever they found themselves short of cash to buy eatables. Anyway, their taste buds and digestive systems were still in shape to enjoy eating anything that they could afford. Still, sometimes they did feel the urge for home food. They would then go to Gursevak's uncle's home to gratify their need. His aunt carried a guilty feeling inside that she had created a situation where Gursevak thought of moving away from the home. His visits gave her a soothing feeling and she did not even mind him bringing Balbir along.

On one such visit, Guru found a comely girl sitting on a moodha (an easy chair fabricated out of reeds). She was introduced to the friends as Sukhvinder Kaur from a village not very far from their own and a student of tenth class in a government high school at Lahore. She happened to be a relation of Gursevak's aunt and came to visit her quite often from her hostel. The girl oozed some sort of freshness around her. With her chiselled features, glowing skin, shapely teeth, shiny eyes, streamlined body and shy smile, she appeared to be an all-season beauty who would look pretty, even if some make-up artists were to put her in clothes of sack and make her to wear an oily look or even if she woke up on a summer afternoon with dishevelled hair and perspiring all over. Even while clinching her teeth in anger over something, she would appear to be a fine picture of a woman. She would not look odd even when blowing meaningless kisses all around, as a professional cheerleader.

At least this is how she appeared to Gursevak. Perhaps she was just a homely beauty at the peak of her puberty and not much else. Love, however, makes a person see in someone that others cannot see. Though he pretended not to display any excessive interest in her, he did not miss any opportunity to have a furtive look at her on the sly. An inner voice seemed to have whispered to him, 'Look no further. She is the one.' His life was never to be the same after this. The frequency of his visits to the house increased. He would drop in on some excuse or the other. She had also managed to shed her initial hesitation in talking to him and a regular channel of communication had opened between them. Now, he was Guru for her and she was Sukhi for him. First, they talked about their folks back home, the lands they owned, the crops they raised, bulls and buffaloes they had and so on. Then they moved towards discussing their school/college life and the freedom movement. Gradually, they started opening up about themselves. Finally, inch by inch, they started uncovering their inner feelings of liking and love for each other.

The vibes between them became more and more noticeable with the passage of time. Balbir was in the know of what his friend was up to right from the beginning. This had rather become an unending topic of discussion between them. His aunt was the next to pick this up on her mental radar. On one hand, she was careful to ensure that the young couple did not get too close before their marriage. She did not allow them an opportunity to even hold hands. On the other hand, she was happy about the goings-on at her place. It gave her an opportunity to take credit with the parents of Sukhvinder of finding a suitable match for her settling down in life. Her hostel, in any case, would not allow them to get anywhere near each other. So the love between them remained confined to stealing some moments to see and talk to each other at his uncle's home. Even this bit of togetherness, they looked forward to with great eagerness.

His uncle had already written to their parents about them and they had shown lively interest in the relationship. So, things were quite on course for Guru and Sukhi. However, 1947 was soon on them. Lahore was now fast turning communally turbulent. The two communities were getting increasingly antipathetic and apprehensive of each other. With the power shift in politics round the corner, a vacuum seemed to be developing in the governance of the province and the law-and-order situation seemed to be deteriorating gradually. There were stray cases of rioting and stabbings on the sly.

The situation, however, had still not gone out of control. Guru and Sukhi were thus able to stay on for their annual examinations. After this, they were back in their villages for vacation. The young lovers were sad on their separation and that summer really hung heavy on them. Yet, they had hope in abundance in their hearts. In fact, Guru was able to visit Sukhi's village a couple of times on various pretexts. Her parents did not mind it, as they were themselves keen to have a good look at their prospective son-in-law. Thus, these much-looked-forward-to contacts kept the two in good spirits.

Both had cleared their examinations creditably. It was now time for them to resume their studies in their respective colleges. Concerned for their safety, their parents were quite reluctant to send them back to Lahore. They, however, convinced them that the situation on the ground was not as bad as it appeared at their place. They prevailed on them to let them go in the interest of their careers. Their main agenda, not so hidden from their parents, was, of course, to have an opportunity to be close to each other. Guru thus joined Balbir as a student of BA (First Year). Sukhi was in first year of her FA.

The Subcontinent Splits

❧

The young couple had misread the situation completely. A lot of communal steam had built inside the two communities and Lahore was now rapidly becoming a boiling cauldron. There was an alarming increase in stabbing cases. Groups of miscreants were now always on the lookout with tins of inflammable materials to set each others' properties on fire. There was a 'taall' (firewood depot) right adjacent to the building where Guru and Balbir stayed. The adult male occupants were organized to perform guard duties by night so that the taall was not set afire by some rabid elements from the other community, turning their own building into an inferno.

The All India Congress party finally reconciled to the divisive demand of the Muslim League on the basis of the two-nation theory. Soon, Radcliffe had drawn lines on the map of India to divide the subcontinent into the sovereign states of India and Pakistan. The province of Punjab also got bifurcated along communal lines. As soon as the people got some idea about the boundary between India and Pakistan, all hell broke loose. The ghastly news of a passenger train being stopped en route to Ferozepur and the passengers identified as Hindus being massacred proved to be the last straw to break the camel's back. There was bound to be a chain reaction to this on both sides of the newly marked border. Thus, the holocaust of the Partition started devouring humanity in hordes like a long-hungry monster.

Gurbux had wisely sent his family back well in time. Fortunately, even he was able to get into the last train that could make to India safely. Guru would not leave without Sukhi. He collected his belongings that could be easily carried and left in a tonga for Sukhi's hostel. The hostel staff, in this emergency, did not make much fuss about the girl leaving for safety with Guru. Perhaps they had come to know that he was her fiancé. Both of them left on their hazardous journey to the Lahore railway station and somehow made it to the station safely. There were some security arrangements in place at the station that kept the rioters at bay. After an agonizing wait of about six hours they managed to get into a passenger train leaving for Ferozepur. There was also a sprinkling of Muslim families in the train.

Some Muslim miscreants got into the train at Raiwind. When the train was midway through to Ferozepur, they pulled the chain around midnight as per their plan. Hordes of waiting rioters then surrounded the train and started pulling out the passengers. They posed as if they were the soldiers of God, out on a campaign to cleanse the land of the infidels. They were accordingly shouting the war cries of 'Allah hu Akbar'. In reality, however, they were, at best, the soldiers of fortune who had got a rare opportunity to loot and rape. A nice Muslim couple, sitting next to Guru and Sukhi, was kind enough to produce two abayas (a full-length outer garment for Muslim women) and asked the two to put these on and try to sneak to safety under the cover of darkness. They were thus able to escape to the surrounding fields while most of the Hindu passengers in the train were massacred. It was hazardous to stay for long at the spot as the miscreants also started pouring into the fields dragging along some young Hindu women on whom they were able to lay their hands. Many of them were gang-raped and killed in the fields and a few were taken along for further abuse.

Keeping not very far from the railway tracks, Guru and Sukhi kept moving hand in hand in the direction of Ferozepur. On the way, they found an empty liquor bottle and filled it with water. They must have covered about ten kilometres in the night. Well before dawn started breaking, they found a culvert overgrown with vegetation underneath. They collected some more foliage and went into hiding for the day. Guru had some panjeeri with him that came very handy on the occasion. The place was moist, muddy and emitting stinking vapours. There could also have been an odd snake or two around for company. They, however, thought it would not, after all, be as venomous as the humans outside. In face of the dangers lurking not very far, the place did not feel all that dirty and uncomfortable. They got into an embrace and just went to sleep. The existential anxiety did not allow any urge for sex to build up in their minds, despite their bodies being closely clasped. The idea of clasping together was just to make them into a smaller lump for easier hiding. Strangely, they felt spiritual rather than sexual beings in this situation of nearness.

As they woke up, they heard some people working in the fields and some passing by. This raised their heartbeats, but they kept their calm. At long last, darkness started descending. The voices around them started fading and then falling silent. When it got sufficiently dark, Guru crawled out and looked around. Feeling no human presence around, he whispered to Sukhi to come out. They walked to the fringe of the fields and then resumed their walk towards Ferozepur. After about an hour, they found themselves close to a railway station where a goods train looked like preparing to leave in the direction of Ferozepur. They saw their chance here. Taking cautious steps, they started moving closer. As the guard gave the green signal for its departure, they mounted an open wagon and lay down.

With some hope of making it safely across the newly imposed border, they could now afford to breathe a bit easier. The noise of the train running on the tracks afforded them an opportunity to talk normally. It was Sukhi to open up first.

She soulfully said, 'With you around me I would love to live for one hundred years. But, if Waheguru might so will, I am also ready to die in your lap right here.'

'Do not talk of dying. Death to those sons of bitches who are killing the innocents mindlessly,' Guru muttered pulling her closer.

'But, I suppose this must be happening on our side of the border too,' said Sukhi.

Guru said without much of conviction, 'I do not think so. Our people cannot be so beastly.'

The train took them tantalizingly close to the border. It seemed to be coming to stop at a prominent station. They soon found out that it was Kasur, which the Hindu faithful believed to have been founded by Kush, the twin brother of Luv. It also happened to be the final resting place of the legendary Sufi poet, Bulleh Shah. There were rumours aplenty that the city was swarming with Muslim troublemakers out to waylay the Hindu escapees before they finally crossed over. So, the couple jumped from the wagon as the train slowed down and tried to keep themselves in the hiding as well as they could.

In the morning, they put on their abayas, moved to the platform and sat on a bench at the station. Their hearts missed a beat as they saw a passenger train approaching. The bogies were packed like sardines and even every square inch of space on their roofs seemed to be desperately clutched by the passengers. However, to their great relief, they sighted some Gurkha military men on the roof of a bogie guarding the train. First, they tried to force themselves into a coach. On failing to do so, they mounted the coupling between two compartments and just hung on there as the train moved. After a while some kindly people pulled them up and they just squeezed themselves among them. The time span of just about an hour's journey from Kasur to Ferozepur felt like eternity. The feeling of terror on the faces of the refugees started visibly melting as soon as the border was crossed. However, the misery that they had undergone still hung there. There was not a face that looked at ease.

At long last, the train made it to Ferozepur. The aching bodies started squeezing out of the bogies, dragging along through the crowds whatever belongings they were still left with. Many volunteers were there on the platform with buckets of water and baskets of food. The fatigued and famished passengers did not display any impatience in grabbing the food, as there seemed to be enough food for everybody and enough people to serve it. After having their grub, the passengers started looking for trains to their destinations. Some, of course, had no destination in mind. They nonetheless had a gut feeling that Ferozepur would not be able to take them all. So, they must make somewhere to the interiors of the country.

Guru and Sukhi, now able to breathe normally, also collected a few loaves and cooked dal/vegetable in donas (bowls made with stitched dry leaves). They felt as if they were having proper food after ages. They still had about thirty rupees with them which was a decent amount to take them to their villages. After having a number of helpings like many others, they joined the volunteers in distributing food to others. They even parted with a five rupee note as their contribution towards bringing some comfort to the surviving refugees landing from Pakistan. They now planned to take a train going in the direction of their villages. After learning that the next train for Ludhiana was likely to leave only after about four hours, they lied down on the platform along with many other weary passengers to grab some sleep. Trains kept steaming in and out of the station and the platform remained abuzz with activity and commotion all the time.

When they got up, they found a train overfilled with Muslim passengers leaving for Lahore. The train had some Baluch soldiers perched on the roof of a coach for protection of the passengers. Still there was some splattering of blood here and there to indicate that some passengers had made to the safety of the protected train in bloodied condition. Military men were then held quite in awe on both sides of the border. So, the sight of even a small posse of them on the train roof was enough to keep the marauders at bay.

They got into the passenger train to Ludhiana as soon as it was brought to the platform. From the conversations among the passengers, Guru and Sukhi gathered that there was a big gathering of Muslims from the adjoining areas in a village near a railway station on the way. They had established some sort of a defensive position there to protect themselves. Besides the usual swords and spears, they also had a couple of double-barrel guns. Some Hindu and Sikh freebooters had been planning to overrun this position to seek revenge and out of the lure of loot and gratification of lust. The Muslims were in quite some strength there, so the raid involved some risk. It was learnt that quite a big armed band had mounted this train to carry out the attack on them. As the train drew near, the raiders pulled the chain and dismounted. Once the mob of marauders closed on them, the Muslim defenders opened fire in the air to scare them away. However, this did not work. Rather it misfired on them. The military escort with the train did not perhaps have an exact idea as to what was happening. They immediately opened retaliatory fire into the village. The two muskets with the Muslim defenders with limited number of cartridges were no match to the .303 military rifles. They thus panicked and started fleeing for their lives towards the adjoining fields. Many of them were chased and slaughtered. More were killed in the village itself. Some of their women were raped and killed on the spot. Some were dragged to the train.

A young Muslim girl was brought to the bogie where Guru and Sukhi were seated. She was made to sit on the lap of an uncouth fellow who seemed be the leader of the ring around him. Others in the group started feeling her breasts. A few hands could be seen slithering like cobras up her thighs to explore. Finding that crying in the situation was of no use, the girl had gone numb with fear, though she was writhing in utter agony at her body being so ruthlessly violated. Guru and Sukhi were ashamed to see her plight. It was Sukhi who dared to protest, 'What the hell are you people up to? Are you not left with any sense of shame inside?'

The half-enraged, half-amused villains shouted back at her indignantly, *'Kudiye, chupp kar ke baithi raih, nahin taan tainu be sodh dayan gey.'* (Keep sitting quietly. Otherwise, you would also be killed by us.)

She wanted to say something further, but Guru stopped her out of concern for her safety. There was no point in arguing with these scamps in the circumstances. So, they just turned their face from the shameful sight and tried to take their mind away. Their thoughts instantly went to the lamenting lines of Wordsworth that they had been taught in their colleges, '...much it grieved my heart to think, what man has made of man.' Many among the evildoers might be of the same view. But, at that point of time, they were in the grip of mob mentality— they didn't know what they were doing.

As the train neared Ludhiana, they pulled their prey down the train even before it had come to proper halt. They dragged her to the nearby farms. Somebody had already lifted her shirt and undid the cord of her salwar while she was being whisked away for obvious gang rape and possibly, for being done to death thereafter. Her tormentors had completely forgotten that she was also someone's daughter. If in his power, her father would chase them up to hell like a man possessed and tear them apart. Some of their own daughters, sisters and wives could be facing a similar plight on the other side of the borders. The gang just seemed to have convinced themselves that they were only delivering justice on the 'eye-for-eye' principle. They did not realize, as Mahatma Gandhi once said, that such an impulse would leave the world without eyes. Guru and Sukhi got down at Ludhiana. They tried to shake off the gory scenes of rape and slaughter near Raiwind and Ludhiana from their mental radar. However, it seemed impossible to do so. It appeared that these would stay planted on their mind forever. They had seen the world at its best and worst during the course of the last few days. Nonetheless, they knew that their parents had no news about them for about a week and must be overwhelmed with worry. They could send telegrams from here, but they felt that they themselves would reach homes well before the telegrams. Dawn was just about to break. They started looking for a train to their village in the flurry of chaotic activity at the station. They learnt that a passenger train would be leaving shortly for the station close to Sukhi's village. The train did arrive after a while, and they got into one of the crowded bogies with hope fluttering in their hearts that they would soon be among their folks, narrating the stories about their ordeal. The train had a number of unscheduled halts due to chain pulling and it seemed to be a journey into eternity for the couple.

Finally, they reached their destination in a somewhat haggard condition. A boy of the village spotted Sukhi, but he wanted to be sure. Soon her brother who made daily rounds of the platform looking for her in all trains both from the direction of Amritsar and Ludhiana also located her. They locked themselves in each other's arms in a tearful reunion. This assured the boy that the girl that he had sighted was in fact Sukhi. He ran towards the village shouting, 'Oae, Sukhi bhain aa gaee, Sukhi Bhain aa gaee.' (Buddies, sister Sukhi has come back, sister Sukhi has come back.) There was a commotion in the village as soon as his shouts registered on the villagers. Her family members rushed out of the home in whatever shape they were. Tears of joy rolled down their cheeks as Sukhi and Guru were seen approaching. They rushed towards them and the family just kept Sukhi engulfed in an embrace for a long while. As they separated, Sukhi, pointing to Guru, told them, 'Bebe, aehana karke hi maen ujj thode samne haan.' (Mother, it is because of Gursevak Jee only that I am with you today again.)

Her parents were already familiar with him and had seen him several times. They were happy to note that their prospective son-in-law not only looked a fine picture of a man, he was a man too. Her father said, 'Chall puttar pehlan ghar chalde haan.' (Let us make it to the home first.) Addressing the gathering of the villagers on the spot, he further said, 'Aeh meri dhee te puttar da nawan janam hai. Tuseen bhi aao.' (This is the rebirth of my daughter and my son. You also come along to our place.) Next many hours were spent in celebrations and listening of the stories of their great escape.

Guru and Sukhi had spent a few nights together. This fact started churning inside many minds as the time began ticking. With this consideration in view, Sukhi's father lost no time in throwing a hint to the gathering that a decision had already been taken by the two sides to marry them. It was necessary to do so quickly so as not to allow an opportunity for tongues to wag. A message was sent to Gursevak's folks accordingly. They rushed to Sukhi's village to see him. The occasion was also utilized to conduct their engagement ceremony. Soon afterwards they were united in marriage to the relief and comfort of the couple as well as the two families.

Life Starts Anew

In those days, marriages were traditionally solemnized in this part of the country quite early, sometimes in the childhood itself. However, these were just in the nature of a formal commitment between the two families. These were allowed to be consummated only after the married youngsters came of age. Another ceremony, named as Maklaawa (meeting) was held on the occasion to signify that the young husband and wife were now free to launch their sexual life. As the day of Maklaawa drew nearer, the boy would be joyful over the prospect of having the first look at and the access to the hidden areas of female anatomy. The young wife would also equally look forward to a new life with a loving lifetime companion who would open the gates of sexual pleasures for her. However, her thrill would be usually intermixed with a few apprehensions over her treatment in the new home and the pain on the occasion of consummation of the marriage.

On the occasion of Maklaawa, the groom is sent to the bride's place for bringing her to the matrimonial home ceremonially. She is allowed to go with the husband after a tearful parting over the knowledge that the things were not going to be the same after she departed for the second and the final phase of her life. After all, from now onwards, she would acquire an entirely new identity and belong forever to a new family. Nonetheless, this sadness eventually starts melting into satisfaction over the feeling that an important duty has been done by the nature. Now her parents were just anxious to have the news how their girl was doing at her new home. For this, a new ceremony of Phera (return visit) has been provided for. The bride thus returned to her parental place shortly after the Maklaawa for her folks to learn first-hand as to how she felt among her new relations.

The bride's return after her nuptials is a good source of learning as well as titillation for her female friends, especially the unmarried ones on the cusp of puberty. This is the age when something starts stirring inside their bodies and virginity starts appearing as something itchy. What holds them back then is the social pressure and the awareness that these pleasures may lead to pregnancy, often with deadly consequences. Nonetheless, the curious girls try to coax and cajole the bride to disclose her experience in intimate detail—how she was approached, how she was felt, what she felt about it and how the night finally ended. Thus, starting with the preliminaries they wish to know about the final act.

The shy ones hold back the crucial information of main interest to the surrounding females. Some are, however, themselves keen to relive the blissful moments of their nuptial encounter and open up to narrate everything bit by bit. Typical conversation between these giggling girls runs something like this: 'Then what happened?' Some shyness and redness on cheeks, followed by exasperation and boldness, 'Yes, he then started feeling my breasts like a baby.' A naughty voice rises from a corner, 'Did you feed the poor baby well?' Covering of faces, pouting of mouths in wonder, quickening of beats in young hearts all around and sensation in some groins, but the remark gets the instant response towards course correction, '*Dekho, kaisi besharam kudi hai.*' (See, what a shameless girl she is.)

While quite a few giggles are still emanating from the room where the girls are gathered, some elderly lady barges in, '*Nee hun chhaddo bi bechari noo. Hore kinni der chimbadeeyan raho giyaan?*' (Girls, now leave the poor thing alone. How long would you keep clinging on to her?) This is how the young girls ripen for sexual experiences later in their lives. Otherwise, there is no source of formal sexual education open to them. Even their mothers and elder sisters cannot brief them on this issue beyond a certain point.

This practice of allowing young girls to interact with the brides after their Maklaawa has quite some social wisdom behind it. If not for this interaction, these girls may feel awkward, uncomfortable when their husbands start fiddling with their bodies on their own nuptial night.

Guru was now around nineteen and Sukhi had also attained the age of puberty. They were, therefore, considered grown up enough for Maklaawa. Besides, they were already quite familiar with each other. The ceremony was thus performed without much delay in their case. With this, Sukhi moved to her new home with Guru in a gadda (bullock cart), leaving sobs and tears behind. There were three more people in the cart. However, Guru and Sukhi were made to sit close to each other. There was a piece of fabric covering them together up to their waistlines. So, they were able to hold hands unnoticed. Sukhi once even pressed his hand slightly to convey to him that she felt totally comfortable with him, as she thought that they were, in fact, made for each other. This feeling of oneness made him feel heavenly. For others in the cart, it appeared to be a journey unto eternity. As for them, they wished to continue like this forever. They hardly noticed when they reached their destination.

At her new home, Sukhi was received in all fondness. Both her mother-in-law and father-in-law appeared to be so affectionate that she felt that she had got a new set of parents. With her moving in the home, entered some new traditions, new words and phrases of conversation, new ways of doing certain things, new dishes, new tastes and even new thinking on certain issues in the family. She also learnt many a new things and developed new tastes in her matrimonial home. She was generally regarded to be a cut above the new brides entering the village community lately. She was educated, gentle, good-looking, respectful, and seemed to have a natural capacity to charm herself into people's heart.

Day one got consumed in ceremonies related to the customary familiarization exercises for the couple—quite unnecessary in their case, of course. Still they went through all these games patiently with great gusto. Finally, they were spared of the unwanted attention and company and it was time for them to meet in privacy at night. Two beds were made on the terrace for the purpose, though everybody knew that they would need only one till the first light in the morning.

As the darkness and calm descended and rest of the family was hoped to have fallen asleep, Guru moved to the cot where Sukhi was sitting. He straight away went into the second embrace with her—the first being the one under the culvert on the Lahore-Ferozepur railway line. The fear had then frozen their natural instincts. With all the congeniality and the social approvals in place, she felt a woman now, soft and warm as a rabbit. Softness was understandable, but her face carried some sort of a fragrance also—mild, but highly agreeable. His hands slowly started moving on her. From here, the nature took over. After all, God is keeping the universe going primarily through the instruments of love, sex and gravity. Besides, Plato and Philo (contemporaries of Jesus Christ) believed that human beings were androgynous to begin with. They got separated into unisexual halves (i.e. male and female) at some evolutionary stage later. Probably, this view was picked up from the biblical belief that Eve was born out of the rib of Adam. For this reason, the two halves carried an inborn urge to merge into each other through sex.

Nonetheless, in the case of Guru and Sukhi, sex was not the baring of bodies alone, but the entire being. They may have fiddled with their own private parts out of curiosity or even for pleasure, as is natural with youngsters. However, in the matter of proper sex, they were both, for sure, first-timers. So, the act was performed in a rather unskilful manner. Yet, they felt heavenly about it. It was a sweet and sacred experience in their lives. The rest of the night was spent in talking about how they felt when they saw each other for the first time and the ordeal that they had undergone during the partition of the subcontinent. Then they switched over to what they wanted to make of their lives together.

The first thought in this area went to continuing their education. They decided that soon enough they would seek their parents' permission to join colleges at Ambala where they had a relation settled. Their talking was, of course, interspersed with soulful hugs and kissing which led to sex for the second time. Once was enough to learn and now they were fully knowledgeable about each other's bodies and what they wanted from each other. So, they were able to make a better job of it this time. They thus remained in conversation with each other the whole night. As the dawn started breaking, Guru went to his cot to pose, as if nothing had happened between them. Both were able to snatch an hour or so of sleep, till they were woken up by their folks.

After a couple of days, Guru took Sukhi to her village for the ceremony of Phera. Her parents and curious friends were waiting for them eagerly. The first few hours were spent in welcoming them and serving sweets procured from the nearby town and some delicacies from the village itself. Then Guru was whisked away on the pretext of showing him around the village and the farms owned by his in-law's family. As soon as he was gone, Sukhi was taken inside a room for being debriefed by her mother. When she learnt from Sukhi first-hand that she was happy and content in every way, the mother felt relieved of all worries.

It was now the turn of her female friends to surround her

for information of their interest. The eager girls got chirpy without losing much time.

'We heard that yours is a love marriage. What is it like?' rose a voice.

'Yes, he loves me,' Sukhi confessed.

'How does he love you?' the girls asked in exploratory mode.

'Well, he cares for me a lot and is with me in everything. We feel good and radiant in each other's presence,' Sukhi disclosed.

However, the gathering was after some juicy news. So, some more searching questions followed to bring her to the desired point. Sukhi, however, was too sober a girl to lay bare all her experiences before them. Still, she knew very well what the girls were dying to know from her. She did not disappoint them totally and did satisfy some of their youthful curiosities remaining within the bounds of modesty. She dwelt more on affection than sex.

'Yes, he respects my body and womanhood,' she admitted. The girls looked a little confused. They thought that the husbands did something different with their wives' bodies.

'I think husbands rather love their wives' bodies and that too till these are lovable,' mooted one lady to explore her further.

Sukhi did not oblige the gathering further. Yet, what Sukhi conceded did go some way to meet their hunger for the news. In any case, her friends knew what sort of girl Sukhi was. So they did not expect much from her in the nature of the usual confessions of a bride. Her philosophical saying that her husband respected her body, that what was natural could not be obscene and that without the involvement of mind and soul, sex was only a joint masturbation, just went over their heads and they did not find these funny enough. Nonetheless, it was at least reassuring for them that marriage could be blissful on counts other than sex also. They quite knew that the sexual pleasures were, of course, transient and the romantic urges waned rapidly with time. After all, no sensation could be felt with the same intensity time and again. It was heart-warming for them to know that there could be something more subsisting too about the matrimonial relations.

Most of the brides did not speak well about their mothers-in-law. Some boasted in length as to how they were finally able to outsmart them. Sukhi spoke about her mother-in-law in glowing terms. This was a revelation to many—so, all mothers-in-law were not the nasty beings, as they were generally made out to be. There could be some real good ones around also. They found this revelation reassuring. Husbands were also generally perceived to be dominant and high-handed fellows. Wives often ended snubbed and even thrashed when they tried to be defiant before them. Maidens, thus, subconsciously started looking for some female power to descend from the heavens to stand by their side to enable them to achieve parity with their males. For this reason they developed natural faith in many 'Mata Ranis' (goddesses), quite ahead of the males who had preference for gods.

The session with Sukhi took them on a somewhat different learning trajectory and they ended up warmer in their hearts and wiser in their heads. They seemed to realize that Guru and Sukhi had been able to carve out a life on a somewhat higher plane and they could be followed as role models for ensuring a more meaningful married life. Thus, when the elderly ladies finally intervened to terminate their gossip, they dispersed thinking optimistically about their own future.

Everybody felt good about Sukhi's Phera. Her parents were particularly happy that Sukhi had adjusted well in her matrimonial home. It was now thought prudent to let the couple take charge of their future. Thus, when Sukhi sounded them about continuing their education, they readily agreed. Sukhi was back with Guru to their village after three days. They had missed on their studies for quite a while. So they did not lose any time in seeking the permission of their parents to resume their studies. Their folks had by now started placing high value on education and were thus quite supportive of what the couple had decided.

Balbir joined a degree college much closer to their village at Kapurthala. The Grewals (Guru's family), however, had a relation residing in Ambala. He approached to extend them the initial help to settle down. The hassle involved in seeking enrolment and finding suitable accommodation were smoothly overcome. Guru would have liked to join the D.A.V. College that had shifted from Lahore to Ambala City. However, since it was not a coed institution, they had to seek admissions to a coed college at Ambala Cantt. Guru had enjoyed staying with his friend Balbir at Lahore and Sukhi also remembered the good times that she savoured in the hostel there. However, setting up the first home for them appeared to be an unworldly experience.

They already had with them two sets of durries, quilts, cushions, bed sheets and pillows, besides some utensils, crockery and cutlery as their marriage gifts. The very same day, they were out to purchase a cot, a pressure stove, a chakla (circular wooden board to roll dough), a belna (rolling pin), a tawa (circular pan to cook roti), kerosene oil, vegetables, atta (wheat flour), pulses, tea leaves, sugar, salt, condiments, vegetable oil, buckets, mugs, toiletries, etc. Their landlord maintained a buffalo. They arranged for procurement of milk from him on daily basis. Thus, they set up their kitchen to cook their first meal. They started with preparing tea for themselves and felt good having it together, looking at each other. Sukhi kept some potatoes to boil when the stove was still on and then they got busy with preparations for attending college from the next day.

In the evening, Guru peeled the boiled potatoes and onion, while Sukhi kneaded atta. They did not yet have arrangement for grinding the onion into a paste. So, the onions were just chopped finely and fried in some ghee, salt and condiments. Once the mixture was half-fried, bits of potatoes and tomatoes were put into it. As the vegetable was ready, the tawa was put on the stove to bake about a dozen rotis. Thus, their first simple dinner was ready and they enjoyed having it together. About a quarter seer of milk was put in a utensil to solidify into curd for the next morning. Thus, another sweet home came in existence and their household took a smooth start to last a lifetime.

The next day started with cups of tea, followed about an hour later by paranthas which they savoured with dahi (curd). They had decided to skip lunch and instead do some snacking in the college canteen. They walked to their college and parted company for a few hours to make to their respective classrooms to resume their studies after the long break. Just like them, there were some other students in their classes who were back for studies after a long disruption caused by the Partition. The college was quite considerate towards them and the teaching staff willingly worked extra time to help them cover the backlog of their syllabi.

Carrying proper lunch in a tiffin carrier posed a problem. However, after a while they started carrying packed lunch with them which mostly consisted of paranthas stuffed with mashed potatoes or some grated vegetables or baked with the flour mixed with daal left over from the earlier meals. Sometimes they carried vegetable biryani or simple rotis along with some vegetable cooked dry, like potatoes, stuffed bhindi, shimla mirch and karela, etc. They would have their lunch together sitting in a quiet corner of the canteen. With love in their hearts and young taste buds in mouths, every dish tasted great to them. After following their lunch with a cup of tea or a glass of lassi, they were ready to move to their classrooms to resume their post-recess studies.

Both of them being young and at an impressionable age, loved to see the movies. There were four movie theatres in the city. The cheapest ticket was still available for five aannas. However, this class in the theatres always had some rowdies around. Though the presence of the well-built Guru by the side of Sukhi was quite a deterrent for the loutish characters, still the couple did not feel very comfortable viewing the movies with them around. So, they decided to switch over to the higher ten aanna class which was mostly patronized by the middle-class gentry. The limited money at their disposal meant seeing less number of films. This prompted them to seek part-time teaching jobs in a private school. Two hours' of work in this institution started yielding a welcome sum of sixty rupees a month to their kitty. Though this meant quite a strain over them, it made them feel freer. They could now watch more movies and also afford to visit some restaurants occasionally. Life was a bit busy and strenuous, but they were enjoying it.

The loved and respected ones are initially seen in a different light, as if they are not humans but some higher beings. For instance, we like to think of God as a radiant-looking human male, but we would never bring ourselves round to imagine Him sitting on a commode as all of us do. Even if such a thought flashes in our mind, we would quickly drive it away. The holy Quran duly realizes that if there is an input, there has to be hopefully some output also. The hoories (heavenly damsels) described therein though do not defecate or urinate, they still discharge the output from their bodies in the form of perspiration which also carries an agreeable fragrance. Similarly, to begin with, Guru and Sukhi also saw each other as different beings from another universe, with everything about them being good.

In course of time, they realized that they were also after all the earthly beings who perspired, coughed, sneezed, yawned, belched, farted, blew noses, had bad morning breath and sat on the potty like normal human beings. Their private parts that once carried a sense of mystery about them, were still important as these, besides yielding intense pleasure to each other lay in their exclusive proprietary domain. Otherwise, these were not all that nice to look at. Their sexual sensations were also weakening with each passing day. In fact, no sensation of any sort can be felt with the same potency even for the second time. However, when sexual thrills start tapering off, a sense of commitment to each other starts strengthening in case of true love. The good thing about the couple was that they still found themselves liking and loving each other as normal human beings, even after they had descended down to the earth eventually. They did argue and even quarrelled occasionally, but quickly realized that they had caused discomfort to each other and felt sorry for it. Thus, the rough edges got quickly rounded and life became silken smooth again.

Sukhi was sweet-tempered, but she would not allow any boy to come too near to her. She was fully conscious of the fact that Guru was too jealous a lover to bear with anybody taking any sort of undue interest in her. They had a world of their own and did like the hustle and bustle around it, but no intrusions into it. Mostly, they had to be approached as one single entity. A goddess-like face, the dignified way Sukhi behaved and the simple manner she dressed herself in, were deterrent enough for the boys carrying within them any sort of ideas of taking liberties with her. Moreover, everybody knew that she was a happily married lady and could not be a game for romance. Besides, she had a sturdy escort in Guru to keep the potentially mischievous at bay. So, they did not have any problems on this count in college. Rather, they were a well-regarded and respected couple. Soon enough both of them developed friendships in college and life became even more joyous and meaningful.

The Bonds:
Destined to Last a Lifetime

❧

Vishnu Kumar Kaushal was born in a well-to-do family in the village of Utmanzai near Peshawar which was then the capital city of the North-West Frontier Province of British India. This was a border region with lawlessness and turmoil in its genes. A culture of vendetta and violence was very much prevalent here among the fiercely freedom-minded Pashtuns. Yet there was hardly any communal tension at the place. The province was predominantly Muslim and had just about a sprinkling of Hindus and Sikhs, despite it once being a part of Maharaja Ranjit Singh's empire. Nonetheless, all the communities were comfortable with the presence of others in their midst.

It is nothing short of a miracle that this very boiling cauldron gave rise to one of the greatest worshippers of peace, Abdul Ghaffar Khan, lovingly known by many other names like Bacha Khan, Pacha Khan, Badshah Khan and Frontier Gandhi. He fought relentlessly in the cause of freedom of his land in the peaceful manner of Mahatma Gandhi. Being thus a thorn in the colonial flesh all through, he and his followers, the Khudai Khidmatgars, suffered terrible torture at the hands of the British. Abdul Ghaffar Khan was staunchly opposed to the partition of the subcontinent, and, in fact, lamented that his land had been 'thrown to the wolves', when much against his will, it became a part of Pakistan.

Despite being as devout a Muslim and loyal a citizen of the newly carved-out nation, as anybody else could be, his love and affinity with India and the Gandhian principles was always seen as something irksome by the rulers of Pakistan. The region, now called Khyber Pakhtunkhwa is still not adequately reconciled to the neighbouring province of Punjab that dominates the politics of Pakistan and its mysteriously antipathetic attitude continues to be a cause of worry for the Pakistani government. Perhaps, the tribals of the area feel that they have not been justly treated by the people of the plains. Tolerance of injustice is certainly not in their genes.

Now, returning to the time of Vishnu, his family was living in peace at their village located otherwise in the turbulent land of the ferociously independent warlords. Their family peace was terribly devastated when some lawless elements intruded into their home one night with the intention of robbery. They would have quietly gone away with their loot. However, as ill luck would have it, Vishnu's father happened to wake up and so did the others with the commotion. Some resistance that the robbers got in the home infuriated them no end and they mowed down everybody in the family, except Vishnu. Perhaps, they thought that the baby was too small to be of any help to the police in the matter of their identification and thus he could be safely spared.

After a few hours, the police of the area was at their door looking for clues to get at the ghastly criminals. The bodies were sent for post-mortem and the kindly SHO took the wailing baby in his care for some time till his naani (maternal grandmother) arrived at the place from a village in the vicinity on receiving a message about the bloody incident. While the police was making an all-out effort to work out the crime, the old lady did not know for a while what to do. Worried about the safety of the baby in her arms, she ultimately decided to shift to Kapurthala where one of her other daughters was settled after her marriage. The formalities of settling the issue of Vishnu's guardianship took some time. But her being the natural guardian in the situation, helped to sort out the matter quickly. Once she got permission to deal with the family properties now devolved on her grandson, she hurriedly disposed of everything at throwaway prices. Simultaneously, she also wound up her own establishment at her village post haste and made for Kapurthala with the baby.

She spent a few days at her daughter's place at the princely town as a sort of paying guest. As their family tradition did not permit her to be a burden on the matrimonial household of her daughter, she soon purchased a house for herself. This house could additionally provide for two tenants. The lady brought up her grandson with the help of a small family pension from the British government, some income from her tenants and interest from her investments in the post office. She did not have to feel much financial stringency in maintaining her establishment. Fortunately for Vishnu, she lived long enough to see him mature into an intelligent young man, capable of facing the world by himself. She had by now dedicated almost two decades of her life to make him stand on his own two legs.

She had a bit of a smile and shine on her face in her last hours indicating a sense of satisfaction over doing her duty by her grandchild well. Moving her hand on his head tenderly, she weakly whispered, 'Time now for you to take charge of your life. God be with you.' At this, Vishnu's eyes went moist and there seemed to be a lump in his throat holding him back from words. Yet his look turned into a sort of prayer, as if to beg, 'Naani, please stay on. It is still early for you to leave me alone.' She closed her eyes on the world nonetheless, leaving a tightness and urge to cry somewhere deep within him. He felt lost for a few days, but he had bit of a philosopher inside him who told him that no bravery was involved in weeping. Immortality was after all the preserve of the Divine Being alone. In case of man, even his memories had a limited shelf life. She was both the father and mother to him. However, rather than crying over his loss, he would do better if he could, in some way, ensure that the memory of this loving lady lived on long enough. Later in his life, he was to write two books that he duly dedicated to her memory. He also wrote around two hundred short stories where she seemed to blink time and again.

He was in the second year of his post-graduation when she died, but she had laid a solid foundation for his coming life. She not only left him with the means to sustain himself but also with a will to come good in life. His locally based aunt showed up at his place as periodically as she could for emotional and other help. He also visited her family occasionally. This did give him a feeling that he was after all not alone in the world. But largely he lived independently, managing his own affairs, like handling the tenants, taking care of his investments and cooking his food.

He was quite used to living alone, but had entered an age when girls look lovely and fairy-like to the boys and they start looking for one to live their life with. Vishnu was a talented young man with a flair for writing and acting. While still a student he wrote a number of scripts and acted as a leading character in a number of plays in his college. By the time he finished with his post-graduation, he had emerged as a local celebrity of sorts with quite some fan following in the city. Highly placed people of the area, including the members of the royalty, were among his admirers. It was during one such performance that a lovely lady with Bengal background, by the name of Prema, got attracted to him. Both fell for each other and hurriedly decided in their minds to be life partners. Some sort of communication and platonic liaison was established between them, but it was too early in the day for them to get united. They were firstly too young for marriage and also Vishnu was yet unsettled in his career to take care of their married life. They were otherwise steadfastly sincere in their attachment and wise enough to wait patiently.

Thus, the decision not to look any further had been made by them and the desire to live together had taken deep root in their hearts. Both were strong-willed individuals. So, it had to be a matter of time only. Vishnu was already a bright student. The desire to be one with Prema further invested him with motivation to do well in his final examination. He started working extra hard with his preparations and finally passed creditably, securing a good position at the university level. He tried hard for the job of a lecturer in the government colleges, but could not make it within the time frame in his mind. He did have adequate merit alright, but otherwise nobody to push his case. Besides, he neither had the accommodative conscience nor even the capacity to pay bribes for the purpose. However, he did land the job of a junior lecturer in a private college at the place on a salary of ₹125 per month. He already had the means to sustain him. His salary came handy to build on his savings for the marriage on his mind.

After around two years, he had become quite known for his creative talents in the academic circles. This brought him a lucrative offer to join as a lecturer in a coed college at Ambala Cantt on a decent salary of ₹200 per month. That meant shifting from the place where he was well-settled, but the added attraction with the new offer was that Prema's family had, in the meanwhile, migrated to Kalka, a semi hill station close to Ambala on posting of her father as the postmaster there. That made him make up his mind quickly and he joined on his new posting without any second thoughts. The college helped him in hiring a two-roomed house on a moderate rent of ₹15 per month. He, a young man then, did not mind a little running about to settle down at the new place. He had already brought beddings, a pressure stove, cooking utensils and other essential equipment from Kapurthala, which helped.

On weekends and other holidays, he would quietly slip away to Kalka to meet Prema. Though he rarely visited her family, her folks knew what was churning in these two young minds. Vishnu always tried his hand at Bengali when in their company and often made a mess of it. However, her family had picked up some fondness for the genial and accommodative nature of the Punjabi young man. When at Kalka, Vishnu had made it a point to stay in a guest house overlooking Prema's residence, so that he could get a glimpse of her as often as possible. Sometimes, they were also able to exchange a few words with each other on the sly. Her parents were getting increasingly agreeable to their alliance. After all, Vishnu was a good picture of a man—well-educated, nicely settled, well-behaved and always prepared to adjust with the Bengali way of life. Prema also had learnt to speak Punjabi, and, in fact, she made a much better job of it, having spent quite a few years in Punjab already.

Another three years went past. Prema had also graduated now from Punjab University in first division. There was no hurdle in the way of their marriage now. They tied the knot in a simple ceremony in which just a few members from the family of Vishnu's aunt, his college mates, family members and some friends from Prema's side participated. There was hardly any fanfare. The world went its way, as if nothing had happened. However, for the eager lovers it was a world-shaking event. They felt as if they had landed on the Moon, the way Neil Armstrong was to do years later. Vishnu had abiding faith in a Mata temple nestled in the grandeur of the Himalayan hills. As soon as the ceremony was over and the guests departed, they made it to the Temple for thanksgiving and getting the blessings of the goddess for a happy and meaningful married life.

As the newly-weds moved to their two-roomed house at Ambala, it started fluttering with activity. They first opened the wedding gifts to take stock of what more they needed to get their household going. Vishnu had earlier thought that he had everything essential that one needed for living a life. Now he realized that he needed many more things to enjoy the bliss and comforts of married life. These were gradually procured to get their shared life moving smoothly on the rails. A comfortable double-bed was felt to be the first necessity. Hardly any time had passed when the cultures and cuisines of Bengal and Punjab amalgamated. The couple was soon speaking the same language, enjoying the same food and got used to the same way of life. They often wondered if they were not one being nestled in two bodies. They also thought that their life partner was not human, but a higher being.

With passage of time, however, reality had to dawn that both of them were very much human and also different from each other on many counts. One of them could not go on adjusting to the other all the time. Both had to learn to adjust to each other in turn. Love, understanding and adjustment were the key, if they had to live together a happy and contented life. They did argue and quarrel occasionally. But their love was deep enough to last at least a lifetime. They also had the wisdom to accept each other finally as ordinary mortals, but certainly the decent ones and the ones made for each other.

Professor Vishnu had instantly become popular in his new college as his reputation of being a creative personality had preceded him even before he joined. His colleagues and students found him to be a pleasant-looking and amiable person. After a few months, Prema also got a clerical job in the local branch of a commercial bank. There was thus welcome addition of about one hundred rupees in their monthly earnings. This enabled them to move to a bigger house. Good times look like just flying past you. As the years went by, some green shoots of prosperity began to be visible in their household. The first to arrive was a bicycle. There were not very many motorized vehicles on the city roads at the time. In fact, India was still stuck in the 'Bicycle Age' then. Vishnu was now often seen doing rounds of the city on his bicycle with Prema perched on the upper bar of the cycle frame and Vishnu leaning over her. With two wheels added to the feet, their mobility had greatly improved. Vishnu dropped Prema at her bank and they rode together to their home in the evenings. Bicycle was followed by other status symbols like a radio, gramophone, table fan, etc. Telephones were then considered too much of a luxury and the couple also did not have much need for it either.

From burning of firewood in a chuhla (hearth), they first switched over to cooking on a charcoal angithi (small kitchen furnace) and then progressed to a kerosene stove. Vishnu was now comfortable eating fish, but he was wary of bones and took a lot of time eating a piece. Prema would often jokingly tell him, 'In the time that you take eating a small piece of fish, a Bengali would polish the whole of a crocodile.' Prema, on her part, had developed a liking for sarson ka saag and makki ki roti, karhi chawal, sabut manhan (cooked black gram), gaajar ka halwa, kheer and other Punjabi dishes.

Vishnu was, understandably, put in charge of all cultural activities in the college. It was customary to enact a play in the college every year. The quality of these stage performances improved so greatly under the stewardship of Vishnu that the prominent people of the city who earlier attended the shows out of social obligation, now looked forward to being invited. He chose highly relevant human issues to build his story around, wrote gripping scripts and catchy dialogues for his plays. He would also devote considerable time and effort on the casting aspect, costumes, rehearsals and stage management. There was thus a carnival atmosphere in the college for about a fortnight every year.

Gursevak and Sukhvinder joined as students after Vishnu had served in the college for around five years. An unearthly sort of bond was established between the two families in the course of just a few months. They were both young couples with not very great difference in their ages. The other meeting point between them was that their love had a platonic beginning and, in fact, it somewhat stayed that way even after their marriages. They did not see their life partners as objects of sex, but as soulmates. They respected the bodies as well as the rest of the being of their partners. Besides, all of them were amiable, lively and genuine individuals, very true to themselves. These were some of the meeting grounds among them. If there were any more, they were yet to know about these.

Vishnu was always ready to devote extra time on his students who had missed on their classes because of the turmoil of the Partition. Guru and Sukhi were among a small group of students who were keen to avail of this great gesture of help with a sense of sincerity and gratefulness. This not only provided an opportunity to these students to make up for the lost time, but also to get familiar with and used to the personality of their teacher. This extra coaching was sometimes arranged at the residence of Vishnu for his convenience. This brought these students in touch with the nicety of Prema also. As far as Guru and Sukhi were concerned, a friendly relationship was forged between the two families, though they never forgot to maintain a certain distance desirable between the teacher and the students.

Sometime in the second half of the academic year, it was time to enact a cultural show in the college. Professor Vishnu suggested that the college should go for a dramatic performance on the martyrdom of Bhagat Singh and his companions who put their lives at stake for the freedom of the motherland. Many of the people were familiar with and could vividly recall the exploits and sacrifices of this brave band of freedom fighters. In fact, a few were a part of their story in some way or the other. The highly emotive theme was to the liking of everybody and all arrangements for its enactment were left to Vishnu. He carried out a painstaking research, worked out what frills were needed to be added for making the show truly fascinating, wrote the script and dialogues. Side by side, he kept scouting for his cast. Though he was not very sure about his histrionic talents, the handsome young Guru did have the appearance of Bhagat Singh. He decided to try him out. He, however, was more confident about Sukhi in the role of the fiancée of Bhagat Singh. Guru was sounded for the role of Bhagat Singh. However, he appeared to be shaky and unsure when told about his provisional selection for the hero's role.

'A great honour, Sir. But I do not think I would be able to

do justice to this role.' Vishnu was prepared for this reaction from him.

'But why?'

'I have never tried my hand at acting, Sir.'

'Okay, but who is asking you to act? Just be real Bhagat Singh for a while on the stage,' Vishnu responded suggestively.

'Sir, I would also have to shave like him sometime midway.'

'Just consider it to be a 'mundan' (the ceremonial clipping of the first crop of hair) of your beard for a patriotic cause. Does anybody blame Bhagat Singh for shaving off his beard? In any case, by the time you go home, you would be wearing this much of beard again. Still, I leave it to you.'

Finding a lingering hint of reluctance on his face, Vishnu told him, 'Okay. We will decide about it tomorrow.'

Next day, he took him and Sukhi to the superintendent of the Central Jail at Ambala City. Handing the invitation card for the college play to the superintendent, he requested him if they could have a look at the enclosure in the jail where the gallows was located. It may not have been possible for the superintendent to oblige them. But the front part of the jail where the gallows complex was located was under extensive renovation and had, in fact, been handed over to the contractor. The operative part of the jail had shrunk to the back. So they were allowed to have a look at the gallows. Vishnu's idea of taking Guru and Sukhi there was to equip and motivate them for their roles.

There was an isolated structure to the right, looking like a jail within the jail. As they entered this triangular enclosure they found themselves in front of the condemned prisoners' cells, each divided in three portions—the cell, a covered verandah and an open compound. Some unfortunate beings must have spent their last days in great unease in these cells, called 'kumhar ahata', till it was time to drag them out to the gallows. The gallows, located in one corner of this triangle, consisted of a brick-lined square pit, with a narrow staircase on one corner for the executioner to go down to deal with the dead or the dying men. On the pit was fixed a sturdy beam on two strong columns on the sides. The beam had three pulleys to deal with three convicts in one go. These brought vivid memories of Bhagat Singh, Raj Guru and Sukhdev, the immortal martyrs of our struggle for independence, rushing to their minds. While it gave a sunken feeling to them that these plucky freedom fighters had to die at the gallows like common criminals, they did not fail to note that they had died a death that many would envy, but few dare.

On two sides of the pit were two hinged wooden boards. These were pulled up and joined together securely with a heavy steel bar with teeth that got pushed into the brackets on the board. These boards, when up and clamped, formed a platform where the condemned spent the last few minutes of their life wearing the hideous noose. The other end of the rope went over the pulley to be tied to an iron beam fixed a few yards behind the gallows. The bar on the platform was connected to a lever which when pulled by the executioner made the planks fall to the sides with a heavy thud. Adequate play was left in the rope for the condemned fellows to fall in the pit and hang there by the neck till death.

After witnessing this awful power of the state to deal with life and death, they quietly walked out, thinking about Nathuram Godse, the assassin of Mahatma Gandhi, who was hanged here. The Mahatma had fallen to Godse's bullets with 'Hey Ram' on his lips. On their way back, they were wondering at the circuitry of the human brain. After all, how could anybody bring himself round to killing a man who wished everybody well? So, Nathuram Godse had to be taken as an arch criminal for assassinating the 'Father of the Nation'. Yet it was also a fact that he did not kill him for any personal gain. You could not treat him as a lunatic either, for he knew exactly what he had done and why. Thus, history has to record the man as a sort of criminal of conscience.

Anyway, the idea in Vishnu's mind had worked. Guru, almost in a state of trance, muttered, 'Sir, I am ready to do Bhagat Singh on the stage, if you consider me fit for the role.' The presence of Sukhi on the stage in his fiancée's role had further added to his confidence.

The other casting for the show was also finalized. The actors for the roles of Kishan Singh and Vidyavati (the parents of Bhagat Singh), James A. Scott and John Saunders (SP and ASP of the British police at Lahore), Lord Irwin (the Viceroy), Mahatma Gandhi, Jawaharlal Nehru and the leading lights of the freedom struggle connected with the episode, like Lala Lajpat Rai, Chandra Shekhar Azad, Batukeshwar Dutt, Shivaram Rajguru, Sukhdev Thapar and many other prominent revolutionaries, were picked up with due diligence. Rehearsals for the drama commenced about a fortnight in advance. The preparations for the stage were also taken up almost simultaneously. Even a contraption like a gallows was set up at the back of the stage to heighten the emotional effects and making the show truly eye-catching.

Guru was a little shaky in the beginning. His expressions and dialogue delivery both needed quite some brushing up. However, earnestness and the will to learn were very much in evidence in him. Professor Vishnu, himself an accomplished actor, was now in the director's role. He worked on Guru with patience till he started feeling that he was good enough to fit in Bhagat Singh's shoes. The powerful script that brought all aspects of the martyr's personality into sharp focus—his revolutionary spirit, socialistic bent of mind, atheism, reformist zeal, vision of what needed to be done in India after the Independence—was to play its own part in making the play a success. All the hard work that had gone into the writing work, stage management and performances duly won appreciation and applause from the distinguished invitees, the college staff and students as well as the other viewers. When Bhagat Singh, Rajguru and Sukhdev were hanged at the gallows put up at the stage, many viewing eyes welled up with tears. Vishnu had also written a soulful theme song for the play which was set to music by some talents of the college itself. The song was to remain on many lips for quite some time to come. The performers, especially Professor Vishnu, Guru and Sukhi, felt very good over what they had been able to do.

After about a couple of months, the final examinations were on them. Vishnu took special pains to see that his wards, particularly Guru and Sukhi, did well. With the examinations over, the college closed for summer vacation. Guru and Sukhi went to take leave of Vishnu and Prema, where they received a very warm and friendly send-off. They then left for their village where Guru's father was not keeping particularly well.

Urge to Do Something Different

U pon return to the village they sensed something was seriously amiss. They were greeted with smiles, but these appeared to be superficial. The smile on the lips did not appear to be symphonic with the sadness in their eyes. The two seemed to be playing a different tune. The truth soon dawned on them as they rushed to their bedridden father. His condition was far worse than what had been conveyed to them. Their folks, in fact, did not wish to distract them in the midst of their examinations.

The village people of Punjab did, indeed, look strong and sturdy in their youth. However, they then appeared to wither quite rapidly. By the mid-forties, most of them developed a paunch which they, of course, considered to be a sign of robust health. Approaching the age of sixty, they started losing their capacity to think and converse coherently. That is how the words 'sathhya gaya' came into circulation in the day-to-day lingo here. These meant that the man had reached the age of sathh (sixty) and had, therefore, quite naturally gone senile.

This, however, was not the case with Guru's father. Despite being on the wrong side of sixty, he was still mentally quite alert, capable of coming up with wise solutions to the problems that cropped up in the household every now and then. His advice was greatly respected in the family and even in the village. Severe illness may have felled him, but he still inspired love and respect. Finding Guru and Sukhi standing stunned by his cot, he forced a smile on his face and tried to convince them that there was nothing much wrong with him. They, however, lost no time to conclude that he needed to be examined by a qualified doctor immediately.

The very next day, he, along with his string cot, was lifted on to a gadda and driven to the government hospital in the nearby town. The doctor there suspected malignancy in his body, but could not be sure about it. He advised him to be shifted to Kapurthala where he was diagnosed to be a case of lung cancer and advised to be taken to the Irwin Hospital at Delhi. Hectic arrangements were made for him being moved to Delhi and for his admission to the Irwin Hospital. He underwent a thorough check-up there and news about his condition was simply shocking. The cancer had spread to many of the vital organs in his body and no amount of chemotherapy or surgery would work in his case. The doctors gave Guru the painful advice that his father's days were numbered and conditions needed to be created so that he was able to spend his last days in as much peace and comfort as possible. He was prescribed ointments and heavy doses of painkillers and was advised to be taken back home.

The patient was thus brought back to the village to spend

his last days among his loved ones. It gave a sinking sensation to the family members that they were to see him dying. But they had to be per force philosophical about the tragedy. Sukhi, Guru and his mother spent most of their time by the side of the dying man, trying to make him as comfortable as possible. All his wishes were attended to promptly as his last wishes. Whenever in pain, painkillers were given to him for temporary respite. After a few weeks, malignancy started bursting on various parts of his torso. Guru and his mother applied ointment over the ulcers to bring him some relief. They could do nothing more about it. In the final phase of the mortal illness, he was found writhing in unbearable pain. Nobody was able to understand what he had done to deserve all this agony. He had done no such thing in this life at least. Unable to see him in this condition, the family again put his string cot on a cart to take him to the hospital. However, he lost the battle against cancer on the way itself and his body was brought back home. By now, everybody was reconciled to his loss. While grieving over his loss, the family did not escape feeling relieved over the fact that there was end to his agony. After all, there was no point in living in that state.

But all said and done, nobody is ever prepared to lose a parent, especially such a loving and decent one. A mysterious emptiness descended at the place with his death. It was difficult for them to believe that the reality—that they had been living with for such a long time—had got lost in eternity and had become an illusion. Every death of a near and dear one spreads an ethos of eeriness in a family and brings the feelings of one's vulnerability in focus. Up till now his next generation nursed some sort of illusion of immortality. They felt that things would remain the same for all time to come. His death made the ultimate reality of life dawn on them. They could now visualize their own bodies being placed on pyres one day, one after the other—it was just a matter of time. Nonetheless, it is a temporary phenomenon. It would, indeed, have been impossible to live our lives in peace and comfort, had time not been a great healer. For quite a few days, some ladies of the village, who almost seemed to be professionals for such occasions, appeared at their place for 'Seeappa' (the traditional breast-beating in condolence). This throng of relations and villagers to their house, however, kept melting with every passing day and the things slowly started returning to nearly what these were before. A death in family, if anything, injected a dose of maturity in Guru and Sukhi. They suddenly felt older than what they actually were.

The time for declaration of the university results of Guru and Sukhi also started drawing nearer. This also helped them to shift their attention from the tragedy in the family towards the curiosity about their results. The day the issue of *The Tribune* carrying their results was to be collected by the newspaper vender at the railway station close to their village at around 2 a.m., they spent the night on the bench on the railway platform. As soon as the train steamed in and the vendor collected his bundle of the newspaper, they could hardly wait to grab their copy from him. Shuffling the pages impatiently, they spread the sheet containing the result under a lamp and started searching for their roll numbers in a great hurry. Guru's roll number was finally located and he was now a proud graduate, having scraped through in second division on the margin. Sukhi had passed her FA in high second division. Both were happy about their results. After allowing the moment to soak in for a while, they thought of Balbir. The bright fellow was expectedly found to have passed his BA, securing first division marks.

It would have been a big celebratory occasion in the village over the results, but for the recent tragedy in Guru's family. Nonetheless, village folks made a beeline to Guru's house to convey their felicitations. Guru and Sukhi themselves went to Balbir's house to congratulate him. After the excitement subsided, everybody in the family started thinking what was to be done next. The first thought went to their benefactor Professor Vishnu. They would go to Ambala to express their gratitude to him. But what about continuing their studies?

'Bebe Ji (mother) and the farms cannot be left alone in this situation. I have done my graduation while you are stuck midway. So, I stay at home and you continue your education for the next two years,' Guru suggested to Sukhi.

'I would stay with you wherever you are,' was her instinctive response. There was not much time on hand to convince her. So, Guru broke the conversation there.

'Okay, Sukhi, we shall decide about it later. In any case, we have to wind up from Ambala and we must also see Professor Vishnu and Prema Ji before that. We not only owe a big debt of gratitude to them for the help and encouragement we received, but also for the affection and interest that they showered on us.' Sukhi readily nodded in agreement this time.

❦

Once at Ambala, they made it straight to their tenement and then the same evening to their professor's house. Both Vishnu and Prema already knew about their result and were happy about it, but the news of the death of Guru's father gave them quite a jolt. The fact that they would not be able to continue their studies at the place made them feel all the more sad. Guru and Sukhi fumbled for words while trying to express their emotional gratitude. But their eyes said it all—how deeply they felt about their patronage for their career and how sad they felt parting company with them. However, they felt truly elated when Vishnu and Prema expressed a desire to visit their family to convey their condolences in person. This was duly fixed up and, true to their word, they landed at their village just after a few days.

Everybody in the family and even in the village felt good about it. After all, some highly learned beings, living a life on a much higher plane, had chosen to visit their village. The family felt that the expression of condolence by them was not merely a formality—the concern seemed to be real, coming from somewhere deep from their hearts. They were shown around the farms, the school and the panchayat ghar, etc. and served various delicacies of the village like the lassi, cane juice, makki ki roti and sarson ka saag. This made them feel good. After soaking in the freshness and leisurely ambience of the vastly spread fields under open skies, the couple felt that it was time to return to their normal routine. Before taking leave of the family they did not forget to thank everybody profusely for their warmth and affection. They also proposed that at least Sukhi should continue her studies, as she was in a neither-here-nor-there situation. This clinched the issue.

A lot of adjustments had to be done to admit Sukhi in the BA course in a residential college, not very far from their village. A mai (an elderly maid) was engaged to be a helping hand to Bebe Ji in household chores. Besides tending the farms, Guru took over some of the female burdens like giving bath to the family animals and bringing fodder for them. Guru made it a point to visit Sukhi often in her hostel. When in the city, he would take her around for meals and movies or just for outings. Sukhi would also come to the village on weekends and vacations. While there, she would promptly engage herself in domestic work to share household burdens with Bebe Ji and Guru. She would carry meals for the husband to their farms and carry load of charhi (fodder) on her way back. And yes, they also had their love nest deep into the tall growing crops of cotton, charhi and sugarcane where they could spend some intimate and joyous moments of their lives.

Two years thus flew. Sukhi returned to her village to be with Guru and Bebe Ji. After around another two months, it was time for the publication of the BA/BSc results of Punjab University. Sukhi and Guru again spent the night on a platform bench of their railway station to grab a copy of *The Tribune* from the vendor as soon as the train arrived from Ambala when it was still dark. The newspaper was again spread under a lamp post to rummage through the pages hurriedly to locate the ones containing the results. At long last the impatient couple located Sukhi's roll number. She had passed creditably in the second division. A lot of load suddenly lifted from their minds, though they did not know for quite a while how to savour the moment. Guru looked around and when he felt that nobody was watching them, he grabbed Sukhi in his arms. They remained in tight embrace till they realized that somebody may drop from somewhere to see them entangled. Ultimately, hand in hand, the two proud graduates returned to the village to announce the good news to the family and friends. There was a flutter all round over the village bride doing them proud.

The couple finally settled to the life pattern of their ancestors. When his farms needed to be ploughed or levelled by running the phatta after the seeds had been poured in the furrows, Guru would go to the farms early in the morning with a plough on his shoulders and the pair of bullocks in front. Sukhi would carry lunch for both at noon. The set of utensils that Sukhi brought the meals in and served the lunch in had gone a little sophistication. The items of lunch, though basically not very different, had also undergone some change in line with the tastes that they had developed while living in Ambala. They would sit in privacy in their love nest, deep in the farm, have their lunch, talk about their farms, family and future, lie in each other's arms for a while and often end up making love.

The ethos in the home was also not very different, except for the fact that they had started subscribing to an English newspaper and also often read the books of their interest that they had accumulated. Otherwise, their time was mostly spent in taking care of domestic animals and other household chores. The monotonous routine did not go well with what they had bargained for. However, Guru, as the head of the family now, had a responsibility to discharge by the family, particularly to see that Bebe Ji did not feel forlorn in the absence of their father. They never gave a hint that they were not happy as farmers. Quite a few years went by. All this while, Guru often opened his heart to Sukhi that he was not happy doing farming.

'Sukhi, do you really think that we bargained for this pattern of life. Our degrees are of very little use in this line, as we did not study subjects related to agriculture. As far as farming is concerned, we are still illiterates.'

Sukhi was quite in agreement with her husband. She, in fact, added, 'As we have learnt, with two-thirds of the country's population engaged in agriculture, this sector contributes just about one-sixth to our gross national product. One eventually gets what one produces. So, the farmers are doomed to remain poor, if this equation continues to persist. The country has to somehow find ways and means of ensuring that sizeable number of people move out of farming and those who remain are enabled to produce substantially more from their farms. Nothing else would work to improve the farmers' lot.'

'Exactly, Sukhi, I wish to be one of the first to move out, as I do not have my heart in farming. The openness and freshness of the farms fascinates me, but the fact that I have very little to contribute, disturbs me.'

'Anyway, Guru, let Bebe Ji not have a hint of what we feel inside. This would hurt her deep within.'

'You are right, Sukhi. But let us keep it in a corner of our mind that we are to do something about it at some appropriate time.'

This is the way their discussion on the subject often ended.

Both of them had an incipient desire for change inside. They wanted to live their life differently.

❦

Balbir was keen on a career in police and also wanted to have a decent start in the line. With his first-class BA degree and hardworking nature, he could have well taken a shot at the Indian Police Service, but he could not bring himself round to think that big. In fact, there was nobody at hand to guide and pep him up for this high-grade competition. So, he set up a self-imposed glass ceiling over his head that he would try only for the subordinate position of a sub-inspector of police instead. He made several attempts and went past the stage of written test twice, but fell at the final hurdle of the personal interviews. This gave him a feeling that complete absence of any recommendatory support at his back could be coming in his way. This could well be true or just a suspicion born in his mind out of frustration.

Balbir finally got a job of auditor in the accounts department of the Bhakra Nangal Project. The job did not satisfy him because he was not of a fault-finding nature. The God-fearing young man was also not interested in the usual cut from the contractors at the stage of scrutinizing their bills. He now realized that even the job of a sub-inspector of police, which seemed so attractive from outside, may also not have suited his nature. All this set him thinking about the better alternatives.

Many young people from nearby villages had migrated to the United Kingdom. Upon returning to their villages on vacation they usually talked in exaggerated terms about the quality of life in England. That put stars in the eyes of those listening to them. Balbir had an acquaintance, Iqbal Singh Maan, who had recently returned from the UK. He got in touch with him.

'Migration is not all that difficult. Visas for permanent stay are easily available at this point of time. Some curbs are in the coming. So, if you have migration in mind, go for it straight away. I shall take care of you till you settle down there,' Iqbal briefed him.

This made Balbir make up his mind. The most cumbersome part of the exercise was the obtaining of the passport. He got it after some wait and running about. Visa for the UK, as Iqbal had said, did not pose much problem. He managed some money for the airfare and his initial stay in England and was finally ready to leave for London. His bosom friend, Guru, accompanied by Sukhi, gave him a warm send-off. It was not easy in those days to remain in touch with the people settled abroad. Letters took ages to reach and telephone calls, besides involving too long a wait for comfort, cost a fortune. These friends, however, managed to remain in communication all through and they kept on giving updates to each other on regular basis. After working as a factory labourer for some time, Balbir got the job of administrative assistant under the British Government. He later got promoted as administrative officer in around two years' time.

Guru and Sukhi were lying on their backs in their love nest watching the open sky and talking as usual. They were unmindful of the people working in the adjacent fields, secure in their belief that others knew little about their place of privacy. That proved to be their illusion. A boy from their neighbourhood came running to them straight to startle them with the news that Bebe Ji was not well. She was, indeed, a little indisposed when they had left her at home that day, but there did not appear to be anything seriously wrong with her. Both of them were jerked out of their reverie. They immediately arranged themselves and rushed towards home. They found Bebe Ji lying motionless with her eyes closed, surrounded by some ladies from the village. As they shook her gently, she looked weakly at them, while assuring them there was nothing much to worry about her. But her general condition said something else. A gadda was made ready in a hurry and she was taken to a civil hospital in the neighbouring town. Her condition deteriorated rapidly on the third day and she passed away within a few hours. Ever since their father had expired, the kindly lady had looked lost and a little disoriented. She seemed to have been left with very little will to live and appeared to be in a hurry to join her husband. Her death was, in a way, her prayer being answered. Nonetheless, nobody is ever ready to lose a mother, because life is never the same after she departs. Guru and Sukhi also had a feeling of emptiness for a long while. However, after the funeral and other rites were over and they gradually came out of the shock, they suddenly realized that they were now free to explore options as to what they could make of the rest of their lives.

First, they thought of giving their lands on lease and try for civil jobs in the nearby cities. Then, Balbir came to their mind. He seemed to be beckoning them to join him in England. Eventually, the lure of life abroad caught up with them also and they made up their mind to migrate to have a look at what the world beyond our borders was like. Balbir was contacted to convey their decision. He was expectedly happy over it and offered them to stay with him, till they were able to set up their own home. They collected a decent amount of money by disposing of their farmland, secured their passports after some effort and had visas for permanent settlement in the UK stamped on these, fixed their air reservation and thus another family from Punjab was ready to leave for what it thought was a land of opportunity. As usual, many of their relations and almost the entire village gathered at their place to give them a send-off. Guru's uncle undertook the responsibility to take care of their house and some of the close relations accompanied them to the Palam Airport at Delhi.

The Sublime Will

T he nursery set up by Guru and Sukhi was now thriving and they had a fairly flourishing business in flowers, potted plants, seeds and manure; they had also picked up some expertise in raising bonsais. One had to be a really dedicated learner, with loads of patience, to master the fine art of cultivating bonsais. Both Guru and Sukhi were not in any way lacking in perseverance and tenacity. Once they took up a project in hand, they went like persons possessed to ensure its successful execution. This, in fact, was the secret of their success.

In the beginning, the couple went through the literature related to the growing of the bonsai plants. Bonsais were raised from the normal seeds only, but the process required meticulous care and delicate handling like that of newborn babies. The plants first needed stratification of the pot with soil mixed with grit at the bottom and a layer of standard bonsai soil on the top. Seeds were sown about an inch below the top. The grit in soil helped in draining of the surplus water. The best season for sowing was autumn. Once the plants grew up, these had to be trimmed with great care continually. This chipping and chopping required a lot of professionalism. The tenacious couple again proved themselves equal to the task that they had taken in hand, and after years of effort there were rows and rows of bonsai pots in their farm. These had good demand in homes, offices and shops and fetched a decent price to compensate for all the skill and labour that went into their raising.

The potted bonsais brought them further prosperity and pounds started pouring in more rapidly. This enabled them to purchase some more adjacent land to extend their nursery and do up their farmhouse for a more comfortable stay there, whenever needed. The financially comfortable couple now started getting further ideas.

'Why not start some training programmes in raising various trees, flowering bushes and potted plants, particularly the bonsais and creepers, dear?' suggested Sukhi.

Guru responded thoughtfully, 'Yes, my dear. Good idea. This would not only bring us some cash, but would also yield us some side benefits. It would make our sales pick up and in the process of the practical training we would get some extra hands for our help in the farm too.' They were, indeed, picking business sense fast and becoming financially wise.

❦

It was round about this time that they got a call from Vishnu who seemed to be making up his mind to migrate to England. There was always some sort of unearthly vibe and a sentimental connect between the two families. Guru and Sukhi somehow always carried a feeling that they owed something to their erstwhile teacher and his wife for the love and encouragement showered on them. Guru thus jumped with excitement on the prospect of Vishnu and Prema joining them in England. The enthused man readily offered them all the help in settling down here and also gave him tips on how to go about it.

That helped Vishnu make up his mind finally and preparations got under way for their journey into uncertainty. Once they got their passports and the visas got stamped over these, he bade goodbye to his college and collected his terminal dues. Vishnu was a highly popular figure in his college. Many of his colleagues and students thus made it a sentimental parting and a few tears also welled up in some eyes. Vishnu, also, could not stop himself from getting emotional. After all, he was not only parting company with his colleagues and students, but also bidding goodbye to the country where he was born, had breathed and been brought up; where his grandmother had taught him to face life and the world and where he had found his love.

Household stuff and even ornaments had to be disposed of to raise money for the tickets and have a few pounds in pocket. The family was now practically left with just one worldly possession, their house at Kapurthala. A feeling crossed their minds that they had burnt their boats already and there was no going back from here. For around a month till their departure, they felt themselves to be living the Arabian Nights, full of excitement as well anxieties. They really lived the month on edge. Finally, it was time to take the plunge.

Needless to say, Guru and Sukhi were truly euphoric over the prospect of hosting their erstwhile benefactors and soulmates from India. They soon started making preparations to receive them and making them comfortable in England. They already had the idea in their mind of starting a school to launch a training programme for those interested in growing various plants. It occurred to them that Vishnu, with a vast experience and ability as a trainer, could be handy here. However, they could not bear their honoured teacher to be their employee. Yet, the first thing to be done was to make their guests feel settled, keeping in view the fact that they were highly self-respecting people. They would welcome help from them for a while but not reconcile to live on charity for long. They had to make them feel that that they were on their own as quickly as possible.

'I have something churning in my mind', Sukhi muttered.

'What is it, my dear? You are so good at troubleshooting,' said Guru.

'Vishnu Sir is so good in organizing and communication skills. Why don't we offer him the task of raising our training institution as our partner. He may not have much knowledge of floriculture, but we have got so many books on the subject. He is quick in uptake and his ability to pass on his learning to others is undoubted. Then, most of our course content would consist of practical training. This is where we can move in,' Sukhi suggested.

'I think you are absolutely right. See, you have solved yet another problem of ours. We could sure go about it this way. This settles it,' said Guru reacting positively to her proposal.

There was still a month for the Kaushals to land in England. Sukhi had been getting her periods regularly. This time, there was an extraordinary delay of ten days. When this came to the notice of Guru, they rushed to a clinic with hope in heart. It got confirmed that at long last Sukhi was pregnant. The next day, they were prostrate in the Southall gurdwara for thanksgiving. A decent number of pounds were poured in the donation box there. They had been waiting to hear this news for years now. Within days that they learnt that Vishnu was coming to them with family and they had committed themselves to extend him earnest help, their prayers were answered. It occurred to them that this could not be a mere coincidence. They thus started seeing some sort of sublimity in their relationship with this family.

There was, of course, a fine chemistry or a meeting ground between the two families. They carried a feeling inside that they had been together with their present life partners for ages and would remain so even in the next life. But it was for the first time that Guru and Sukhi felt that the two families were also divinely ordained to remain in close touch with each other at least in this life. The Kaushals were, in any case, a good influence in their lives and they wanted their relationship to stay this way.

Guru started taking good care of Sukhi as an expectant mother. He would not allow her to do any arduous work. Earlier, she participated in all sorts of digging work by the side of her husband. Now, pick and shovel were completely out for her. She would just go around her nursery and see if the plants were doing well. She attended to supply orders from the market and homes, did pruning work on the bonsais, took the visitors around their farm and even started planning for their school. Thus, so far as light manual and mental work was concerned, she remained actively involved. Guru ensured that she took timely and nourishing meals, as medically advised. While in bed at night they talked about whether they were going to beget a son or a daughter. They had settled on their names too. During their sleep they often dreamt how their baby would look like. They could hope for the best as both of them were good-looking and perfectly healthy.

While waiting for Vishnu to arrive with Prema and two kids, they decided that they would vacate the entire upper floor, consisting of two bedrooms and a toilet, for their honoured guests and they themselves would do with a guest room on the ground floor. Rest of the house—living/dining rooms and kitchen, etc.—would be shared. In any case, they had started spending most of their time at their farmhouse. They thought this arrangement could conveniently continue as long as their guests decided to stay.

They started looking for some private job for Prema to eventually settle her in a suitable white-collar government job. Balbir was also sounded about it and he was happy to help, as he always was.

Another Journey into Uncertainty

❧

Passports in hand, with UK visas stamped thereon and tickets tucked therein, the family was all set to leave for London to start a new life. Vishnu and Prema, with two small kids in tow, were certainly excited. However, their excitement was intermixed with quite some anxiety, as they faced an uncertain future in the new land. Anyway, they had boldly liquidated all their material belongings to raise money for the immigration. There could be no going back now. With the boats thus already burnt, all that was left to be done was to take their chance. These were the sort of ideas churning in their minds as they stood in queue before the check-in counter at the Palam Airport at New Delhi. Every time they tried to shake off the uneasiness inside, it returned to them hastily back when they thought of the kids with them. After all, they had also put their future at stake.

Palam Airport was then a poor cousin of a host of the renowned airports of the world, but it looked gorgeous to the kids. They had not seen anything more magnificent in their lives as yet. The elder boy, Sunil, around four, was uncontrollably playful, trying to jerk himself free from his father's hold to loaf around in the spacious lounge. The younger one, Varun, just about two, was feeling sleepy, all the while crying intermittently to be carried in the arms of his mother. The two were thus pumping in quite some extra exasperation in the already anxious parents who had taken the plunge trusting their sponsor, Gursevak. They were trying to convince themselves that he would not let them down. But, what if they were?

They had come from a distant town in Punjab and stayed for the night in the house of an all-weather friend in New Delhi. The couple had understandably spent the night tossing and turning in the bed. Sleep that night was not for their eyes, as their minds had a lot to attend to. They were now waiting impatiently in the queue for the check-in. At long last, it was their turn. As the documents were handed over at the counter for being processed, they felt little tightness inside. Knowing that London was a much colder place, they had stuffed a good number of quilts, blankets, shawls and other woollens in their luggage. Thus, they felt somewhat relaxed when the person on duty did not create any fuss about their excess baggage. At least one ordeal was over. They were quietly handed back their passports along with the boarding cards and also the tickets stapled with the luggage tags.

As first-timers, they had to struggle a little with the filling up of the immigration forms. However, both of them were too well-educated to get bogged down by these. Soon they found themselves standing in the immigration queue. As the stamping formalities got over at this counter, they moved towards the

Customs area. After a cursory inquisitive look, the Customs officials just waved them to move on. They then made their way to the departure lounge. Fortunately, there were no security checks then. These were to be inflicted on the world later. Still, the boarding involved waiting for another one hour. With one set of tensions over, they again started thinking of the problems they might have to face in the alien land. Gursevak Singh was supposed to meet them at the airport. What if he did not turn up? They had his address, but how would they be able to afford a taxi to his place with just a few pounds that they had been left with.

The kids, of course, were blissfully ignorant about what was bothering their parents. They had, by now, found a way to entertain themselves by running around the rows of chairs and by playing hide-and-seek behind these. Their hilariousness was quite out of tune with what was passing through their parents' minds. But they were the understanding parents. They could well understood that they could not expect their babies to be on the same wavelength as them and adjust their playfulness to their sombre mood at the moment. They had to run about quite a bit to recover them from here and there, but did not allow their exasperation to ruin the playful mood of the kids.

When the uncertainties ached too much in their hearts, Vishnu and Prema tried to fix their minds on the good things that had happened to them in India and the prosperous times that beckoned them to England. They were certainly not badly off in the land of their birth. Vishnu was, however, bent upon taking his beloved life partner to greener pastures, to what he liked to believe, a sort of freedom-from-want situation. He was thoroughly convinced that she deserved it. Prema, on her part, was always prepared to let him have his way and just follow him through thick and thin. Otherwise, the cushy job of a lecturer in India that Vishnu held was not bad in any way.

Their life had flowed along blissfully till Vishnu started feeling the pinch of ordinariness. The country then was in the throes of food deficiency and roaming in the world with a begging bowl for its teeming millions. This is not what he had bargained for in life. He wanted to soar on to the skies with Prema. Finally, he decided not to reconcile to a life of scarcity and standing in long queues for the smallest of things in his native land. Moreover, deep down in their beings, the absence of struggle in life was making him feel stale. Adventure was badly needed to light up their lives. Thus when he sat in the departure lounge, he very much had a dream in his eyes. But, he was not sure whether things would pan out the way he had planned. Prema, however, always felt at ease as long as she saw Vishnu sitting by her.

After a considerable while, there was an announcement on the public address system for the passengers to proceed to the aircraft. The family lined up for the journey into the future with the boarding cards in hand. Moving slowly, they finally made their way to the foot of the stepladder laid to reach the aircraft that would fly them to the land of their dreams. Earlier, they had seen aeroplanes flying in the air from far and had imagined that they must be carrying some lucky people to some fairyland destinations. Now they were going to be one of them. No wonder, for a while, they felt like Armstrong stepping on the Moon. They hoped it must be some sort of a heavenly experience sitting inside an aeroplane. Once in, the welcoming airhostesses and comfortably cushioned seats responded well to their hopes. However, during the next almost forty minutes when the aircraft was getting ready to fly, they started feeling cramped. The free-breathing world outside was certainly more open, cosy and enjoyable. Here, you needed toffees, drinks, snacks and smiles to feel comfortable. The kids were, however, still joyful and were jostling to get close to the windows. They had seen aeroplanes up in the skies from outside. Now they wanted to see how the world looked from the sky.

As the passengers were accounted for and flying formalities were over, the engines started whirring and produced a jarring noise. A plethora of announcements—which this time they listened to with attention and which during their frequent flights later, were to sound monotonous—followed. The aircraft then began to taxi towards the runway for takeoff. Once there, the engines were suddenly accelerated full throttle and the gigantic aircraft started shivering. Brakes were then released for it to move at a scorching pace for a while and then lift off the ground. The kids saw in wonder the earth and its buildings suddenly going topsy-turvy. Everything on the ground seemed in a terrible hurry to slip by them. They felt themselves in a dream while departing from the earth at such a furious pace. When the aircraft gained height, everything seemed settled a lot more serenely. The earth below now looked like an unfolding map. The next thing that delighted them was their cruising through the clouds and finally the sight of the black-and-white mist milling below them and weaving all sorts of myriad patterns.

Despite a slight feeling of nausea, the family seemed to enjoy their first journey through the air. They, particularly the kids, were highly impressed with the pleasant-looking and sweet-talking hostesses. During the journey stretching over around half a day, they had quite a few servings of drinks, snacks and sumptuous meals. Vishnu and Prema tried to doze off every now and then, but they were too excited and anxious to be able to make up for the previous night's lack of sleep.

'The first thing to be done at Heathrow is to somehow reach Gursevak's home. Hope, he is there,' Vishnu seemed to be talking to himself.

Understanding his anxiety, Prema intervened, 'He will be there. Relax.' Vishnu felt convinced momentarily. However, uncertainty came rushing back to him again. After all, the entire responsibility for their adventure was on him.

He again muttered involuntarily, 'What if...'

'Relax, relax.' Prema cut him short.

The kids, by now, felt that they had seen enough of the swirling clouds and the slow-moving plains down below from out of the windows. So, they started feeling sleepy. After all, how long could you go on enjoying the tearing through the white foam of the clouds or floating above them? They went into quite a few spells of sound sleep and had to be woken up for the meals with some effort.

Finally, the 'fasten seat belt' signs were switched on and there were the usual announcements that they were going to land at the Heathrow International Airport in a short while, about the temperature outside and that the passengers should keep sitting till the aircraft came to a complete halt, etc.

Soon they found themselves hovering over London. They had imagined the city to have a look of something like Disneyland. But, what they saw below were orderly rows of ordinary houses, looking like clusters of army barracks. As the aircraft touched the ground with a light thud unfamiliar to the first-timer family, tension returned to them.

Vishnu's lips whistled again, 'Let us see.'

Prema was still composed. She said, 'Let us leave it to God and Gursevak.'

The aircraft still seemed skidding on the airport turf when some impatient passengers started getting up from the seats and opening the easels to get hold of their hand baggage, as if they had been uncomfortable sitting inside and wanted to leave in a hurry. However, there was no melee-like situation, the eager passengers just filed up to leave. They found a few hostesses lined up near the exit point to bid them farewell and hoping that the airline would see them again.

Vishnu was keen to follow the other passengers closely so that they did not stray into a wrong area and lose track of what was to be done next. After the immigration and Customs formalities were over, they flowed on to recover their luggage. But more than their luggage, they were anxious about Gursevak.

❧

It was time now for Guru to leave for Heathrow Airport to receive the Kaushals who were likely to land there in about an hour's time. Sukhi had decided to stay back as they knew that it would be difficult to adjust everybody in the car with the considerable amount of luggage that Vishnu must be carrying. Then she also had to keep lunch ready for them.

Vishnu and Prema were eagerly looking for a face in the crowd. They wondered whether they would be able to recognize it from a distance after so many years. However, it was Guru who located them first. Flailing his arms vigorously, he raised a low shout, 'Here, Sir'. As Vishnu noticed him waving at them animatedly, a load was off his mind straight away, because he could read the warmth on his face. The exuberance on his face declared that all was well for them. They now started feeling sorry that they had unnecessarily entertained some lingering doubts about the sincerity of Guru. Guru also eased out of his eagerness and raised his hand in welcome when he saw them waving back in response. They tried to rush towards each other instinctively, but could not come very close because some barriers between them at the place had still to be crossed.

Formalities of immigration and Customs check over, Guru joined them and reverently touched the feet of his former teacher and Prema. While they got busy in collecting their luggage, he tried to hold the kids in his arms. They, however, squirmed to get loose, taking him to be a stranger. But they were to soon feel that he was the most amiable and loving uncle. On coming out, the family ran a first look at London. It appeared to be fresh, clean and orderly. They then emptied the luggage trolleys into the car and squeezed themselves in. Looking around all the way to Southall, while occasionally exchanging a few words with Guru, what churned in their mind was, 'so, this was the London of their dreams, very much worldly but a lot different from their own country... Why could their country not be like England.' They were to later learn that Englishmen also felt why England could also not be like India in certain aspects, family values, for instance. Here, life partners did not come with a lifetime guarantee. At the time when the partners took the pledge, 'Till death do us apart', they wondered within how long their partnership would last. Back in India, the matrimonial life may not necessarily be a happy one, but the bonds nonetheless subsisted through thick or thin for at least a lifetime. These two families were representatives of this Indian ethos. What was preferable between a free and liberated life and a committed one, was a debatable issue.

In about half an hour, the car was passing by a row of houses that appeared to be similar and finally stopped at one where the Kaushals were to spend a few years of their lives, till it was time to move into their own house. They found an eager face waiting for them there. It was Sukhi. She also respectfully touched their feet and got into a soulful embrace with Prema. All of them then got busy in unloading the stuff in the car and taking it to the first floor where the Kaushals were to live. After this, the two families sat in the living room for a while where Guru again enquired how things were back home in their country.

Vishnu matter-of-factly disclosed, 'The things were on the upswing, but *wahi chaal bedhangi, jo paehle thee woh ab bhi hai.*' (The disorderliness that prevailed earlier, is still very much there.)

This pointed to the numerous administrative weaknesses of the country, as a result of which the progress was too slow for people's comfort. Sukhi knew that discussion on this issue could extend indefinitely. So she changed the subject and asked them if the flight was comfortable.

'Yes, of course, all went well,' responded Prema.

'In any case you must be feeling jet-lagged after the long flight. I shall serve lunch. After this you relax for a few hours before we resume our conversation.'

Prema joined Sukhi in the kitchen despite her protests not to bother. After lunch, the Kaushals retired for the much-needed spell of sleep, spreading themselves in their beds without bothering much to arrange their stuff. They got up after a good sleep of four to five hours. The kids were still sleeping. They started unpacking their luggage and placing various items at the right places. This done, they woke up the kids and got them ready to move downstairs to the living room.

Sukhi was then in the kitchen preparing dinner. Prema again joined her for help. While the two ladies engaged themselves in light-hearted conversation to open up to each other afresh, Guru and Vishnu, after a while of pleasantries, came down to the discussions about the plan that Guru had in mind for the Kaushals to find their feet in England.

'Sir, English people love flowers and greenery. That is how almost all the houses have gardens and grassy patches in their backyards. Seeds, saplings, manure and potted plants are quite in demand here. But many of the households do not have adequate expertise in taking care of their plants, especially the bonsais that we have begun raising in our farm. So, we plan to conduct a training programme in our nursery to impart knowledge about raising various kinds of plants and their after-care. I need your help in launching this institution. First, how do you like the idea, Sir?' Guru posed to Vishnu.

Vishnu began with the words, 'First, my dear Guru, you stop addressing me as Sir. I am no longer your teacher, we are friends now. This would enable us to be more relaxed in each other's company. Otherwise, I fully endorse your plan. It is certainly a good idea. I shall go all the way with you in your project and extend whatever help you think I am capable of.'

'All right, Sir. Sorry. I shall comply with your suggestion to bring ourselves round to behave as your friend. But our respect for you would subsist for all time to come. For this reason, I cannot bear with you being my employee in this venture. I, therefore, offer you partnership in this concern,' responded Guru.

'Fine, Guru. It is really nice of you. But despite my fondness for plants, I do not have any knowledge of floriculture or managing orchards.'

'But, you do possess high-quality communication skills to mesmerize your pupils. Besides, you have wonderful capacity to organize. We do have the practical knowledge in this area, but are not very confident of handling the class. I am sure we can fruitfully complement each other in this venture. We already have a lot of written material on horticulture and can place it at your disposal for study. We shall also purchase more books for your help and for being eventually placed in our library. You may take your own time in preparing your lesson plans. Once the trainees leave your classroom, we shall take them over for practical demonstrations and field work with their own hands. They would also see the seeds sown by them sprouting into green shoots and the saplings planted by them growing into plants during the course of their training. We shall be there by your side for help when the brainstorming sessions are organized. I am sure, Vishnu Ji, you would not only be able to handle all this but also make an excellent job of it.'

Guru sounded quite practical and sweetly reasonable to Vishnu and he thought of giving his consent to his proposal. By this time, the two ladies emerged from the kitchen to announce that dinner was ready. The matter came under further discussion on the dining table and Vishnu duly agreed to Guru's proposal. Back in the living room, the discussion now centred round finding a job for Prema. It was decided that she would work for some time in the same bakery where Guru and Sukhi had started their struggle to settle down, till she found a white-collar job, preferably with the government. Vishnu also brought Guru round to accept some house rent from them. He himself had insisted on paying rent to Balbir while they stayed at his place. So, he could not resist the suggestion of Vishnu for very long.

Son-Rise in the Family

Prema duly joined service with the bakery that was within a walking distance from their residence. Pounds on her palm every evening gave her a deep sense of satisfaction that they had got going in the new country. She knew that the situation demanded hard work from them if they were to be on their own quickly. Sometimes, she did not mind working overtime to earn some extra cash. After work in the bakery, she would rush to the kids to know how they had spent their time while she was away. They seemed self-contained in the matter of company in each other's presence, though now some neighbourhood kids had also started fraternizing with them. Sometimes, Sukhi would take them to their nursery and they enjoyed being amidst the greenery, openness and freshness of the farm, with flowers blooming in their pots and bushes and some fruits and vegetables dangling from the trees. The rows of potted bonsais particularly attracted them no end and these miniaturized trees were a great object of their curiosity and amusement. They keenly watched bonsais being delicately clipped and wondered how such giant trees could be reduced to such a small size, as if these were the babies born to the trees.

After spending a few minutes with the kids, Prema would promptly join Sukhi for kitchen work, as very few households could afford domestic help in this country. Prema very well knew that Sukhi was pregnant and she needed to be taken care of. It was her first pregnancy and Prema, having had the experience of motherhood, was in a position to help and guide her. She did all this with loving care. Sukhi was happy to have a caring companion by her side, when she needed one the most. Though they got very little time to spend together and had lot of workload to handle, they hardly ever felt stressed. In fact, Britain was a busy nation and most of the families here could not hope to spend a lot of time cuddled together. Mostly, all the family members were seen rushing out of their homes in the morning to their offices, factories and other places of work after dropping the children at their schools. Flexible working hours, in vogue here, helped them in catering to their routines. Often, weekends were the only time for the families to sit together or go for excursions to unwind.

Vishnu began accompanying Guru to his nursery farm and started rummaging through the books on horticulture available there. As he delved into this literature, he increasingly felt that horticulture was very much an area of his interest. Soon he was devoting earnest attention to imbibe knowledge about what plants could be raised in the local climate; how the soil needed to be prepared for these; what all fertilizers or what sort of manure was needed for various plants; how the seeds and saplings were to be sown; what aftercare was needed for potted plants, creepers, bushes and trees; what remedial action was possible if the plants did not come up well; how to raise bonsais and do the clipping work on these; what amount of watering and sun exposure was needed in various cases and situations and so on. As the course content started taking shape in the light of its objectives, Vishnu started thinking about his lesson plans and relating these to the practical fieldwork in the farm.

In the meantime, a shed had been put up with necessary facilities to serve as the classroom and the required furniture and training equipment were procured. People were now regularly visiting the nursery and they were also provided picnic facilities here. When they learnt about the launch of the training programme some indicated their intention to enrol. As soon as Vishnu felt confident that his lesson plans would be ready in around a fortnight's time, the date of launch was fixed and messages were sent to friends, local celebrities and regular clients inviting them for the inaugural function. The course was to run over twenty working days and was to cater to twenty-five trainees to begin with. The programme was to open with a forty-minute lecture every day, followed up with demonstrations and fieldwork for two hours. It was to end with brainstorming in the class to clear any doubts and collect new ideas from the trainees.

Fees were kept low for the inaugural course and twelve people had already enrolled for the programme by then. Five more joined by the launch date.

'Not bad to begin with,' Guru and Vishnu seemed to say

to each other, while exchanging looks after all the arrangements were in place.

The inaugural function was attended by a good number of people and it was diligently managed. Vishnu was very impressive in his address to the gathering. In fact, he had a special knack of making even the ordinary things look important. You give him the dullest of topics to speak on, he would manage to inject high interest into it. He began his address with some thought-provoking words that we were in a 'give-and-take' relationship with the Mother Earth. All that we needed to live lay embedded under its surface or came from its superjacent waters or the air in its catchment. Thus all fruits and flowers that we know of also lie buried right in the soil. We had just to take the trouble of getting these from there. Similarly, all that we discharged went back to earth to come back to us with value addition. Floriculture was an art. All artists tried to communicate not only with the people around but also with nature and God—a musician with his vocal chords and instruments, a sculpture with his chisel and hammer, a painter with his colours and brush and a florist with his soil, seeds and clippers. The gathering went back with some food for thought.

All went well with the training programme too and the trainees who passed out went back happy and satisfied. They were given a sapling each, out of those they had helped in raising, to carry home as souvenirs. The first training programme, expectedly, did not yield them much profit moneywise, but it left behind a wealth of experience for the trainers and enabled them to tie up some loose ends for the next course. The needed modifications were made both in the course content as well as the training methodology. Efforts were made to improve the infrastructure also.

After the accounting was done, Guru apologetically offered half of the meagre profit to Vishnu, who reacted, 'Firstly, dear Guru, one must be prepared to undergo some losses during the gestation period. We are lucky that we were able to make a small profit right in the beginning. We can look forward to more rewarding times in future. Secondly, you have contributed a lot in the form of infrastructure and facilities for training and devoted much more time on the practical part of the training. I do not deserve 50 per cent of profit.'

'I am deriving lot many side benefits from this training regimen, Vishnu Ji, in the form of publicity, improved marketing, working hands and so on. In all fairness, you fully deserve at least half the share of profits from this institution.' Guru thus convinced Vishnu that there was no element of generosity in what he had been offered.

Their academy, being the first training facility of this nature in the area, created quite a buzz around. Trainees started flocking to it from a much wider radius. Regular courses commenced after the inaugural one with an enhanced capacity of thirty trainees and these were fully subscribed. Rather, some candidates had to be often wait-listed for the next programme. The course fee was also revised upward reasonably. The venture now started yielding them decent cash. Guru and Vishnu then started toying with the idea of running an advanced course with a few formally qualified horticulturists on their guest faculty. However, this programme was kept in a limbo for some time, as Sukhi's expected delivery date was drawing near.

In the meantime, Prema was able to secure a government job in the social security department as administrative assistant. This was an important step in the Kaushals' settling down. She was now able to devote more time to Sukhi who needed regular check-ups in the hospital. All seemed to be going well with her. It was Prema now who managed the kitchen and Sukhi helped her with just light household work.

The expected date of delivery of Sukhi was getting very close and it was a matter of any moment now. Finally one night she was seen clutching on the pillows in some discomfort. Prema rushed to her as Guru knocked at their bedroom to tell her that something was happening with Sukhi. Sukhi convinced them that it was only slight discomfort and the time had not yet come. Prema ran her hand softly on her forehead and rearranged the pillows deftly to make her feel comfortable while she was trying to go to sleep. Around fifteen minutes later, Sukhi got up writhing in quite some pain. Her condition sounded the red alert this time and a flurry of activity started in the home. Prema had already kept everything handy for the occasion. She rushed upstairs to get dressed and wake up Vishnu also, while Guru ran aimlessly for a while in all directions, not knowing whether to stay by the side of the convulsing wife to comfort her or to get dressed quickly to rush her to the hospital. Soon he collected his wits and telephoned for the ambulance.

In the meantime, all of them got ready and drove Sukhi to the hospital as soon as the ambulance arrived. This journey towards parenthood filled Guru's mind with a variety of thoughts. Sukhi's pain was causing him discomfort and the prospect of returning with a baby of their own to home, was giving him a feeling of joy of the nature never felt before. Upon reaching the hospital, he rushed to register Sukhi and she was briskly moved to the labour room. She was given a dose of anaesthetics to relieve some of her pain, but this is the pain that every mother has to endure to bring a new life into worldly existence. It took another two hours for the contractions to pick up some intensity. The labour pains became increasingly severe. Each wave of contraction sent Sukhi's face contorting, though she appeared to be in a semi-conscious state. The ordeal left her exhausted. Pains peaked and after the burst of severity, there was the son-rise in the family.

The intensity of pain suddenly subsided, though it still lingered. There was a glow of joy and satisfaction on Sukhi's face as she heard the baby crying. The living lump of her flesh that she had just delivered was whisked away for being cleaned and done up. Finally, Sukhi was also cleaned up and brought to the ward to stay under observation for some time. The baby was placed in a cot by her bed for her to have an eyeful at it. Soon Guru and others were also allowed to move in and have a good look at the newborn. The baby was still sleepy and seemed to be lost in some other world. He would open his eyes for a while and then doze off quickly. So many expressions were passing in a procession on his face. He would sometimes let out a smile and just a moment later he would curl his tiny lips, as if wanting to weep. He appeared to be making up his mind whether he was happy to have come into this world or if he was happy to be in the world where he had come from.

With joy and contentment writ large on their faces, Guru and others instinctively raised their hands skyward to express gratefulness to the Divine Being for this blessing and profusely thanked the hospital staff who had attended to Sukhi. Guru's mind at the moment was crowded with too many ideas and emotions. Finally, he pushed these in a corner and decided that he would first go to the gurdwara to pay obeisance to the Almighty who had given him such an ardently wanted gift. He did go there at the first available opportunity. After lying humbly before the 'Granth Sahib' for quite a while, he got up and pushed generous amount of pounds in the donation box.

As the mother and her baby were absolutely fine, they were discharged from the hospital after two days. Prema and some ladies from their neighbourhood took good care of them for the next few days. Around 20 kgs of panjeeri was prepared for Sukhi. This highly nutritious dish was traditionally fed to ladies after delivery to enable them to recoup their health. A forty-day spell of rest, called the 'chhila' period was considered necessary for her to get back to her normal health. As soon as Sukhi was deemed normal, an Akhand Path (continuous recitation of the Granth Sahib over twenty-four hours) was organized at their place as a thanksgiving ceremony.

Now it was time for the namkaran ceremony. The granthi (priest) suggested that the name of the baby should begin with the Gurmukhi letter Jajja (corresponding to the English alphabet G). Some people close to the family suggested various names for the baby—Gurkirpal, Gopal, Gurinder, etc.

Ultimately, Prema made a lovely suggestion, 'How about

Gursukh. After all, he is the son of Guru and Sukhi?'

The gathering instantly liked the idea, as the suggested name connoted the names of his father as well as the mother. He was earlier nicknamed as Golu for looking robust and round-faced. Thus, consensus evolved that the baby would be their Gursukh. The added reason for this was that he could be continued to be called by his pet name that rhymed well with Gursukh. His arrival truly lighted up the things in the household.

Son-Set of Their Lives

T heir lives rolled on along the routine already established. The nursery and the institution attached to it were doing well and had emerged as a landmark in the area. In fact, with their setting up the shop here, the footfalls in the vicinity had increased manifold. A poultry farm had already come up close by. Somebody was in the process of setting up a piggery farm not very far from their nursery. Some other businesses were seen to be interested in moving up here. The place was thus showing signs of opening up. Consequently, the price of land was appreciating at quite a rapid pace.

Business partnerships, in general, rarely survive. However, the one between Guru and Vishnu continued to thrive, as both of them were open-hearted, honest and sweet-tempered individuals, with lot of goodwill for each other. Prema, in the meantime, had picked up a promotion to the next rank of administrative officer. The Kaushals now decided to buy a house for themselves, as they had collected enough cash in their bank to make the initial payment for the mortgage. With the help of Balbir and Guru, they were able to settle the purchase of the property without much bother. The house was of moderate size, located quite close to Guru's residence. Both their sons were school going now and were brilliant in their studies. They could look forward to a bright future for them. They were otherwise the obedient and affectionate ones.

Golu was understandably the apple of the eyes of his parents. His smile for them was the most precious thing on earth. Even when he discharged mucous from his nose, he appeared lovely to them. His crying might have sounded jarring to others, but their ears heard it as music, though they thought that he was announcing some need that deserved to be attended to on priority. With all the fondness and loving care showered on him, Golu developed a tendency to throw around tantrums on minor issues and started acquiring the traits of a spoilt child. Vishnu and Prema were able to hear the warning bells quite early. But, they were mindful of the fact that he was the only child of his family and was born after an agonizingly long wait. So, certain amount of weakness towards him on part of his parents was perfectly understandable. They threw a hint or two to Guru as well as Sukhi not to look at his wayward behaviour with unseeing eyes and not hesitate to exercise some amount of assertiveness and even sternness to put him on a little orderly course. However, they could not bring themselves round to even being slightly harsh towards their son, who was clearly developing some erratic propensities. They continued to remain indulgent towards him, despite being strong-willed otherwise. The Kaushals could also not press the point beyond certain limits for obvious reasons.

Golu was otherwise an intelligent child and could come good in his life, if some ways and means could be found to put him on the right course. By now, Guru and Sukhi had a decent balance in their bank account. They could afford to send their son to a reputed school, which they managed to do. Golu also felt good in the company of the English boys and always wished that he could be like them.

Time, in the absence of crises, flies rather fast and generations move from childhood to adulthood and then to middle age and old age so speedily that they are left wondering whether they had really lived all those bygone years. If the movement is smooth, you do not feel the speed of life. This is what happened with these two families.

In case of the Kaushals, their elder son, Sunil, completed his doctoral study and with this high degree in pocket, he had no difficulty in settling down both in his profession and personal life. He married a lovely lady from India whom his parents had chosen for him with his consent. His doctorate put him on course for a high-grade career. The younger one, Varun, completed his post-graduation and he too registered himself for a doctoral degree. His parents, however, felt that he had also put on enough years by then and should settle down in marriage. They were able to pick a beautiful and vivacious girl from India for him too. The boy decided not to remain dependent on his parents after his marriage. So he left his studies to join a senior management-level job. Thus, the entire family came to live a happy and contented life. As the two sons got going with their lives and got blessed with children, they wisely decided to purchase independent houses for themselves, before the joint family life could throw up any irritants. They, however, continued to remain a joint family in a 'three houses one home' sort of situation and never felt they were living separately. They were a truly inspirational family in the area that their neighbours admired and envied, despite the fact that they had resolutely refused to dilute their pride in the past, rooted in India.

All was well with Guru's family too. Their nursery, along with the training school attached to it, was yielding them a good amount of cash. They had managed to move to a bigger house and Golu was now studying in a reputed college. They continued to enjoy fabulous relationship with Vishnu's family and were held in high regard by their numerous friends. So far so good.

Golu, however, appeared to be becoming a problem child. A discomfiting streak in his behaviour started becoming increasingly noticeable. His outside environment seemed to have completely overshadowed his genes. He was getting more and more anglicized with every passing year and almost felt embarrassed of being the son of his parents. He felt that they were out of tune with life in Britain and needed to change. It was, however, too late in the day for them to make any more adjustments in their lifestyle beyond what they had already done. They took care to dress properly when they went out of their home and tried to keep to British mannerisms while outdoors. But they wanted to remain relaxed while in their home. They relished having their meals on cot rather than the dining table and were still not comfortable eating with knives and forks. Their place did have the proper décor in line with the British custom, but they liked to perch on the sofa with their feet pulled on it, when they were by themselves. They also had not learnt to speak haltingly with a nasal tinge in their tone and with frequent drags for emphasis in every sentence. Golu was shy of inviting his friends to his home, though some of them liked the affectionate ethos of the place. He always carried an apprehension that his friends may catch a glimpse of his parents doing something silly in their presence.

Many a time Guru as well as Sukhi tried to argue with him about the desirability of sticking on to one's roots and taking pride in one's past also.

But he would retort, 'What roots are you talking about, Dad? These are keeping me tied to one place. But for these, I would have moved much forward, much faster. After all, I am trying to lift the family to the high British standards which you failed to do. You should at least stand by me and cooperate with me.'

Half-amused, half-confused, Guru would say to Sukhi, 'What to do, my dear, some brains come wired that way. He seems to think that he has done a great favour to us by being born in our family.'

'Yes,' Sukhi would say, 'he innocently believes that now it is our turn to meet all his demands. He is far removed from the noble principle, "Ask not what the world has done for you; ask what you have done for the world." Perhaps, we gave him too much latitude to do what he wanted to, too much liberty to think the way he willed and excessive licence to feel the way he chose. He does not seem to be interested in our nursery business either. That, of course, is no problem. Let him chart his own course for his career.'

Guru would go silent nodding in agreement. They had been great fighters all their life, but were now finding it difficult to fight against their own blood.

On yet another occasion, they tried to explain to their son that they had come to settle in England in search of better quality of life and were happy living here. They also loved the English ethos and strongly believed that there were many things good about the English people. It had been their effort to imbibe whatever was good in their society. 'But while doing it, we must believe that there are many things good about India also which the British could gainfully adopt.'

Interrupting them, Golu would promptly join issue with them here.

'I do not think that there is anything good about us. Moreover, you must have heard, Mom, "When in Rome, do as the Romans do."'

'We do try to do here what the Englishmen do, son. But within our own home we also do what the Indians do. Is there anything wrong, if we try to preserve at least a part of our identity that way?' Sukhi tried to argue with him.

The young fellow, however, having been so thoroughly exposed to the Western way of life, really felt embarrassed of his background and everyone and everything associated with it. So, he was totally unconvinced. His parents made attempts on numerous other occasions to see if he could be shifted from the extreme position that he had taken in the matter of English culture, but he would not budge an inch. Ultimately, they stopped discussing this aspect with him.

'Anyway, dear, there is nothing to worry till we are together and then, we shall try to marry him to a nice girl of Indian origin. God willing, she may succeed in doing what we are failing to do about him,' they would often end up consoling each other.

It was more or less clear that Golu would wind up their nursery concern post haste after them and would go for what he might consider to be a higher and more lucrative career. Guru thus thought it prudent to take Vishnu in confidence about the situation.

He, therefore sportingly suggested to him, 'You are my most respected friend and, in fact, the soul of this school. It would no doubt be difficult for me to find your replacement. However, I have a tickle in my bones that neither this school nor even the nursery concern are going to last very long after us. Keeping in view the emerging situation, I feel that it would be selfish on my part to hold on to you. It would give me extreme comfort to see you settled on a more secure job.'

Guru did not have to say this. Vishnu already had a clear idea about what was coming and what he could expect from the errant young fellow. So he was very appreciative of what Guru had proposed. They thus launched themselves to locate the right person to take over from Vishnu. With some effort they were able to find a well-qualified elderly pensioner to be on their core faculty as the head. A few others had already been fixed to give guest lectures in their school occasionally. It was, thus, ensured that the facility would keep running smoothly. All of them now had time on hand to see that Vishnu also got a permanent job. Fortunately, a number of interviews that he went through finally culminated in quite a few options for him. He chose to be a lecturer in a privately run institution. His job was light. He could, therefore, still find some time for periodic guest lectures in Guru's school.

Golu was now about to complete his graduation. His parents thought of sounding him for his marriage. They offered to look for a nice girl for him. He, however, did not seem to like the idea of them picking his life partner, but he did not want to be totally blunt with them either. He rather kept on rejecting the prospective brides that they chose for him one after the other, causing them lot of embarrassment. It was clear by then that he did not have much respect for their choice. In fact, he finally told them that they did not have to bother finding him a bride. He would do it himself when he wanted to. This left them with no alternative, except to pray to God that he, in the end, did not bring some awkward lady home as his wife.

Golu eventually did select a girl by the name of Supinder Kaur whom he had been dating for some time and declared his choice to his parents with an air of finality. They were, however, happy over the fact that she happened to be a good-looking girl of Indian origin and also came from a Sikh family, well settled in England. So they went through the formality of seeing her at her place without any fuss and readily gave their consent, which was, in fact, inconsequential.

Golu cleared his degree examination with fairly good grades.

'Shall we now finalize the date of your marriage?' Guru asked him. He was not sure whether he would oblige.

He, however, said reassuringly, 'As you wish, Dad.'

His words were music to his ears and took quite some load off his mind. The wedding date was duly finalized after consultations between the two families. Lot of festivity, feasting, music and Bhangra/Giddha sessions followed, while whisky and beer also flowed in copious quantity—after all, they were Punjabis and believed in enjoying life to the hilt. In the end, the couple sat together in a gurdwara, surrounded by relations and friends to seek the blessings of Waheguru and to bind themselves in marriage according to the Sikh rites. The bride was received in the matrimonial home in all fondness. Some more ceremonies and festivities followed to make her feel comfortable in her new environment.

Supinder did not mind when she was nicknamed as Sapna in her new family. Except for a little streak of assertiveness in her nature, all appeared to be well with her. Guru and Sukhi did not find much wrong with it. They, in fact, wanted their children to have a mind of their own. Sapna, otherwise, seemed to be responding well to the affection being showered on her and making efforts to gel with her in-laws. However, she was also in the mould of their son and did not have very high opinion about Indian values and ways. Both seemed desperate to merge with the British milieu. In fact, they appeared to be involved in some sort of mental struggle to work towards gaining full acceptability in the English order.

Guru and Sukhi grasped what their children wanted and tried to go with them in the interests of peace and harmony in the family. They thus stopped dining at places other than the dining table, started using forks and knives, avoided drinking water by pouring it in their cupped hands held against their mouths and made it a point to sit on the sofa properly and so on. The young couple were, however, not very satisfied with just this much.

As a reaction to this, Guru finally posed to Sukhi, 'Dear, why do we have to do all this when we are not comfortable doing it, especially when it is not leading us anywhere?'

'Yes, you are right, dear. We have lived our family life so far at our own terms. Let us keep things simple and live in our comfort zone and let these young fellows follow their own course. We do not have to make all these adjustments, fearing that we would eventually become dependent and in that phase of our life, we would need looking after by our children,' Sukhi responded.

In any case, it was becoming increasingly evident to them that they could not rely on Golu and Sapna for comfort in their old age. They had to learn to be on their own. So, they gradually reverted to their old ways. With that, some generational distance started developing in the family and domestic congeniality started becoming a casualty of that. Occasionally, they could not withhold their mind from recalling what all they had done for their child and they now had a right to expect something in return. When this was put across to the children, it was not reacted to very kindly and, in fact, resulted in emotional outbursts. They, therefore, finally decided that it would be wiser for them to forget about all this and learn to live in the present. Life is essentially a one-way journey and you have to constantly adjust to the requirements of your existing situation. They, thus, quickly came to conclude that they could hardly treat their son as an insurance policy maturing in their old age. They were now clear in their mind that they would be relevant only till they were the givers. Once they became the takers, they would at best be tolerated as a burden to be somehow carried, as a social duty or for old times' sake. True, their blood in their son's veins may occasionally impel him to show some affection for them, but most of the time they should be prepared to suffer disregard.

Golu and Sapna were ambitious, but they did not have the will to put in sustained hard work to give shape to the lofty ideas in their mind. Golu would often approach his father to discuss some fancy projects worked out by him and end up asking for finance from him. Guru, though often not impressed with his ideas or ability would give him something, hoping against hope that he might strike gold eventually. In the absence of earnestness and single-minded commitment, he invariably ended up in failure to execute his plans. A lot of Guru's hard-earned money had thus gone down the drain. Golu, however, always wound up nursing a grudge that his effort failed only because of the niggardly financial help from his father.

Golu and Sapna could not, however, think in terms of splitting with the parents because they still had dependence on them. Both had now settled on ordinary jobs that enabled them to bring home too little money to cater to their lavish lifestyles that they had got used to. They knew that if they moved out, they would have to rent a house that would take away half of their earnings. They also had in their mind that the babies that they planned to raise would need caring by the grandparents. So they had to somehow stick on there. Their parents could also never think of throwing them out. So the two generations kept on living together a life of compromise.

Thus, the family spent very ordinary time during the next decade during the course of which Sapna gave birth to two kids—the elder one, a daughter who was now around nine years old, and the younger one, a son, now in his seventh year. Despite Golu and Sapna living with them and their two kids also chirping around, Guru and Sukhi lived with an 'Empty Nest Syndrome'.

The Unkindest Cut of Destiny

Change is the law, rather the life, of nature, the very beating of its heart. Time just cannot be tethered. Wheels of time keep moving relentlessly in one direction. Life thus moves from birth to babyhood and from there to adolescence, youth, middle age and old age in a rhythmic sequence till it is time for it to end up in death. Various thinkers have tried to define this phenomenon in their own ways. One view is that we are like the droplets sprayed up in an ocean through the action of waves. We have independent existence for a short while and then fall back into the ocean to vanish without a trace. Some, however, believe that the soul never dies—it just discards a worn-out body to put on a new one. They thus see death as the phenomenon of renewal.

As far as Guru and Sukhi were concerned, their generation now seemed sitting in the departure lounge of life. First to merge into eternity was Balbir. Vishnu followed him soon after. They participated in their funerals with teary eyes, lump in throats and quite some wrenching in their hearts. After the hospitals certified their deaths, their bodies were handed over to the commissioners engaged by them for their last rites on sizeable payments. These were embalmed, put in coffins, dressed in their best attire, as if they were just asleep. On the appointed days, they were carried to the sanctum sanctorum of a church in a proper hearse accompanied by the pall bearers and followed by a convoy of cars of the mourners, some of them feeling a real heaviness in their hearts and the others just following out of their duty as social animals, thinking that if they don't do it, the others would also not attend their funerals. At the church, space was provided for the mourners to place their wreaths and flowers. The priests of their communities performed their last rites. Their coffins were then placed on spring-loaded trolleys which were moved to the opening of an electric furnace. As the alignment was in order, the mouth of the furnace was opened and the electrically actuated trolleys, on pull of a lever, bumped the bodies into the red-hot furnace and thus, ended their worldly existence.

The departure of these two sincere friends shook up Guru and Sukhi because no ready replacements were available for such friends and well-wishers. The added reason for their shock was that their death had brought their own vulnerability in focus. They could not help being overcome with a feeling that their own end was also not very far off and they should start winding up. The stance of their progeny towards them made them feel all the more detached.

Balbir's children did not have much attachment with Guru's family even during his lifetime. With his death, their link with them first weakened to a formal level and then faded, as if it was never there. Their relationship with the Kaushals was, however, on a different plane—it was too soulful to snap that easily. After Vishnu passed away, it smoothly spilled over to the next generation. Sunil and Varun were to remain in affectionate touch with them all through. Prema was also still around as a great source of solace and comfort to them. Still, their zest for life started tapering off gradually. They had even already started thinking in terms of winding up their nursery business to be able to spend more time close to each other in this final lap of life.

They started spending most of their time in their farmhouse in their nursery because they knew that they would hardly be missed by their children. They themselves did miss Golu, Sapna and the kids, but they had decided not to pour out their affection on them unnecessarily, when they hardly seemed to relish it. They were content to let it stay and simmer inside. Occasionally, Golu also gave some indications of carrying some love and respect for them inside. But it did not have much visibility. So his kids were also not able to get close to their grandparents. Thus, two different streams of lives were flowing in the family, rarely coming close to each other to merge. Not that they were not on speaking terms. They generally spoke nicely and even expressed concern for each other, but something was seriously amiss in their relationship. It was perhaps the lack of warmth and genuineness.

'Mom, you are showing up after a long while. Why? You do not like being by our side?' Sapna would occasionally ask Sukhi. This precisely was the reason. But Sukhi would say, 'No, dear. There is lot of work to be attended to in the nursery that keeps us a little busy. Then, you two also remain quite busy.' These, of course, were excuses for hanging on to, at least, good sense in the family. Otherwise, the generations had drifted quite apart.

Nonetheless, Guru and Sukhi still had the comfort of being together in health. Withdrawing into themselves did not cause much unease to them. But then destiny delivered its unkindest cut on them. Sukhi started feeling a sensation of pain in her lower abdomen. When this began getting more pronounced, Guru rushed her to a hospital for check-up. To their shock, she was diagnosed with cervical cancer. The worse part of the silent killer was that it had already spread its tentacles to many other organs in her body. Cancer is, indeed, a dive bomber. You often get to know of it when it is on you already. They, therefore, felt as if some drone had suddenly fired a missile on them. It was now clear that Sukhi did not have much time on hand. The tragic news did not sink in Guru's mind immediately. He kept on hoping against hope that medical science had gone many notches ahead and ways and means would still be found to get Sukhi out of this crisis. Sukhi was not informed about her condition in so many words, but she was intelligent enough to understand what was what. In any case, they were also not left with much to live for either, except for each other.

Guru knew that Sukhi would now need full-time looking after by him, so that she was able to spend the last few months of her life in some solace. The first thing he did was to initiate action to sell off his nursery, so as to keep sufficient cash handy for her treatment. The nursery area had opened up well and the concern was also running quite profitably. So, its sale brought a decent amount to their bank balance. As soon as this happened, Golu again rushed to him with some project to siphon off some of this money. However, this time Guru warded him off and gave him clear indication that from now on, if he was to do something, it would have to be of his own, because all this money might be required for his mother's treatment.

Sapna and Golu were again resentful that such a big amount was being wasted on the patient who had already been declared terminally ill after several diagnostic tests. However, they were careful to contain their feelings within themselves. Sukhi was now spending her last days in the hospital with Guru by her side all the time. Golu and Sapna also dropped in once in a while with their kids to mark their presence. Golu did sometimes have his eyes welled up over the thought that his mother was leaving him for ever and ever. Sapna and the kids were mostly there out of their worldly duty.

Being alone in the hospital room most of the time gave Guru and Sukhi plenty of time to reminisce over their past. When they talked about their first coming in touch in Lahore, the anxious time spent huddled together as a bundle under a railway culvert on the Lahore-Ferozepur track, the heavenly days spent at Ambala after their marriage, especially enacting Bhagat Singh's play on the college stage, a faint smile would appear on the face of fading Sukhi and she would look as pretty to Guru as she did when he saw her for the first time.

They were getting more and more soulful and philosophical in their conversations with every passing day. They now had plenty of time to discuss the problems of the world and also their own. Visions of life after this one had already started to blip on their mental radar. They generally avoided discussing Golu and the kids, as the topic was deeply hurtful. Still, they could never get them out of their system completely—after all, they were the beings of their own blood.

'You see, dear. Golu once lived in my body as a vibrant sperm. From me, he managed to get to the ovum waiting in one of your fallopian tubes and grew into a baby on your blood and flesh. Yes, he was once a part of us. However on being born, he has become a person different from you and me. As an independent individual, he is entitled to live life in his own way. We should not be over-possessive about him. There is no virtue involved in this. In fact, being over-possessive is being greedy. We have done our duty by the nature. Our children will do theirs,' Guru posed to Sukhi and then looked at her waiting for her response.

Sukhi looked faintly amused and then contemplatively opened up, 'You, like me, are hiding a hurt inside, dear. True, we cannot treat him as our property. But, we had a right to wish that he could display a little sense of belonging to us. He has completely flown off the tangent, as if we are nobody to him.'

Guru said in the manner of a moderator, 'You see, dear Sukhi, nobody can own a life except his own.'

'Don't I own you, dear?'

'Yes, you do own me, because I love to let you own me. Same is the case with you. I own you because you are only too willing to be owned by me. Otherwise, too, we belong to each other more than to anybody else in the world. Still, every person has his own priorities that revolve round self-interest. It is sad that we do not rank all that high on the list of priorities in Golu's mind. That is about all. Otherwise, he does carry a fair amount of affection for us within.'

'No, dear. Life is not completely centred around "self". You place my comfort far above yours. You have nearly turned your back on the world for my sake, though I am already on my way to the world next and am unable to do anything for you. I think that if you had been in my position I would have also made any sacrifice for you.'

'True, Sukhi. We are only too willing to make sacrifices for each other. But, even an act of sacrifice is motivated by one's own happiness. I undergo some discomforts for you, as doing so gives me a feeling of comfort. Similarly, we underwent some discomforts for Golu because doing so gave us happiness inside.'

Sukhi nodded in agreement this time, but asked, 'Okay, dear. But, are the children not expected to do their part to let their aging parents feel still relevant, wanted and useful or should they just have their eyes fixed on getting gratis their estate, built on their blood and sweat?'

'They are, dear. Dutiful children do look after their parents, but some don't. Let us face the fact that when someone turns a "taker" from a "giver", his status in life gets downgraded. He has to be from then onwards carried as a burden from the past. Moreover, the times are changing. People have begun thinking that bearing and bringing up children is no guarantee of comfort in old age. It is something that may or may not work. It is a lot better to become self-reliant, at least financially—the way we fortunately happen to be. We should stay that way.'

They had already started bringing them round to detach themselves from their progeny as there was nothing much to look forward to from their son and his family. In fact, they had come to conclude correctly that immortality was the Divine preserve only and it was not meant for anybody else. Even man's memories had a limited shelf life. They knew that their memories would not live very long. Yet, they felt consoled that their story of love for each other would get repeated again and again, with them assuming different names.

After trying all diagnostic tools and examining various possibilities of treatment, the doctors came to the unfortunate conclusion that Sukhi's condition was incurable and her days were numbered. They were finding it difficult to muster suitable words for explaining her condition to Guru, but finally they gave clear indication to him that she was, in fact, destined to die an agonizing death in a few months' time. Something straight away died in Guru at this horrendous news. The next instant, he stood before God in his mind to ask Him as to what they had done to deserve this.

However, he collected himself soon as it was awfully necessary for him to know from the doctors if anything could be done to ensure that she was able to die as painless a death as possible. What he could gather from them was, that Sukhi should be moved in the more congenial atmosphere of home to spend her final days among her folks. This brought a surly glint in his eyes for an instant, but he kept on listening attentively. He was advised that, as of now, she did not have to remain confined to bed and she could move about a little. They equipped Guru with painkillers, ointments and other over-the-counter medicines for use on her. Lastly, they advised him to stay close to a hospital, properly equipped to handle emergencies that her condition might cause often.

So, she was taken home that was big enough to ensure that her condition did not cause much inconvenience to others. For some time, Golu and Sapna tried to be dutiful and spared some time for them. But after they knew that this was to continue for quite some time, they started showing signs of fatigue. Still they kept going through the motions of being the caring children. Guru would take Sukhi to the greenery in their backyard and they would move about tending to the plants or just watching the chirping of the birds on their trees.

They were following with great interest that a pair of turtle doves was trying to set up home on a tree. The birds excitedly flew here and there to collect straw for their nest. Once the nest was ready they settled down there cosily. After a few days, three tiny eggs were seen in the nest. While the female stayed there, the male bird flew errands around and brought provisions home for both of them. Next, they saw some commotion and soft chirping of their offspring. The parent birds now started flying away from their nest to feed themselves and bring food for their offspring. The tiny fellows would eagerly raise their beaks to receive the worms and grain brought for them. They seemed quite happy being fed that way and would have liked to stay in that position all through their life. However, after about a month the parent birds felt that they had done their bit and it was time now for their babies to be on their own.

They tried to coax the reluctant fellows out of the nest, but they tried to pose that it was too early. The parents, however, persisted. One of the young fellows while being pushed out of the nest fluttered a little and fell on the ground with a thud and raised a cacophony to convey that it was yet too young to be asked to be on its own. The parent birds, however, did not find this funny and raised cacophony of their own to tell the young fellows in no uncertain terms that this malingering on their part was not going to be tolerated. The lazy fellows were then left with no alternative than to make an effort. They fluttered out of the nest and settled on a lower branch. They then turned their necks left and right to have a good look at the world outside their nest and then flew away. Guru and Sukhi noticed from the window that that night the nest had fallen silent. Next day, the parent birds also flew away.

'So, this is what life is like. It is just one-way traffic. These birds, having done their duty by the nature, had just forgotten what they had done and endured for their young ones. So should we, Sukhi.' Sukhi just went contemplative for a while and then nodded in agreement.

Sukhi's condition started worsening rapidly. Now, ulcers had started appearing all over her body and these pained. However, she was pained all the more when she once overheard a conversation between Golu and Sapna.

'See, how Daddy dotes over Mummy, though she is in a hopeless condition riddled with ulcers all over and you just do not bother about me,' she appeared to complain.

'Then, what do you want me to do? I should not attend to my dying Mummy even this much?'

'I do not say that. You have to understand that their presence in this condition is not very good for our children. It may lead to some psychological problem with them. Let us face the fact that even we are feeling fatigued. Why don't you persuade Daddy to move Mummy back to the hospital. We could go and visit her there.'

'Okay, darling. I shall speak to Daddy. I also think that Mummy would be more comfortable there.'

However, before a reluctant Golu could speak to his father about it, Sukhi spoke to Guru, 'Would you, dear, fulfil a wish crossing my mind? I wish to die in India.'

'I would take you anywhere you wish. But we have to be close to a proper hospital. There is none close to our village,' Guru explained.

'We could perhaps stay at Ambala or better still at Chandigarh itself where the Post Graduate Institute of Medical Sciences (PGI) is located. I have special fascination for these areas where we have spent some of the best days of our life,' Sukhi suggested.

Guru had to meet this little wish of his heartthrob at this final phase of her life. So, he got in touch with some friends in Chandigarh and Ambala. They were able to locate a newly built furnished flat at Mohali meeting their requirements. Soon they were on their flight to New Delhi and from there to the Chandigarh Airport. Golu and Sapna went through the motions of persuading them to stay on in England. But there was no stopping them once they had made up their mind. Golu's eyes welled up again at the Heathrow Airport when a thought stabbed him that he would not see his Mummy again. He, however, steadied himself by deciding that he would also follow them to India once they settled down there.

The Last Lap

❧

The flat did not pose them many problems. It had water, electricity and essential furniture, including a double bed, sofa set and dining table and a small refrigerator. Guru saw to it that it was made livable for their purposes without wasting much time. They had taken care to bring along some essential items of daily use. Some more were purchased locally. They were now able to prepare tea, coffee, boil milk and heat up their food ordered through a tiffin service. In fact, they had not been left with very many needs in life. Sukhi just wanted to die in peace and Guru wished that she should live a painless life till she was alive. Anything beyond that was a bonus.

However, even these little things that they wished for were not written in their destiny. Guru was to spend most of his time ferrying her to the PGI again and again when her pain became unbearable and applying ointments on her ulcers. Sukhi oscillated between relief and pain like a pendulum. She had the deceptive sensation of relief when under sedation. But she always knew that pain would return to haunt her after a while.

The only real relief was the presence of a caring Guru by her side. Their companionship had now deepened to the surreal limits. This is what love was really meant to be. Anything short of that was something else, not love.

A brave Sukhi, who had fought valiantly against the travails of life so far, finally lost nerve and came to conclude that there was only one answer to her agony—death. Her exasperation had to do something with not only her own excruciating pain, but also it was over the discomforts that Guru was undergoing for her. She had urged for euthanasia to the doctors several times. Even Guru had agreed to put her to a peaceful end in view of her extremely painful condition that was totally irreversible. However, the doctors could not comply with their request because euthanasia was certainly illegal and that would have amounted to culpable homicide under the law. Sukhi was thus driven to desperation. She wrote a note when Guru was away for a while, explaining her undying love for Guru and the way he had written off the world for her sake. Then she wrote in clear terms that she was taking her own life because she could no longer bear the agony of her condition. She placed the paper carefully under her pillow.

In a soulful moment when her pain had just started shooting, she asked Guru, 'Dear, can I ask you to fulfil another wish of mine. I assure you that this was going to be my last one.'

Guru earnestly responded, 'I am prepared to give my life for you, my love. You just ask for it.'

'It is going to be tougher than that, darling. You have to take mine and relieve me of my unbearable pain,' said Sukhi in a tone that sounded like something not from this world.

Guru looked stunned and had no words to react.

Anticipating his reply, Sukhi further said, 'And give me a word that after me, you would live your natural life. I have loads of patience to wait for you in the next life.'

Guru did not respond again. Soon her condition started deteriorating rapidly. Her face started contorting with excruciating pain.

'How do I look now? Do you still love my ugly self?' She managed to ask summoning the final bit of strength in her.

Guru now melted, 'My love, you still look as lovely as you looked when I saw you for the first time.'

'Then, kill me.'

With that, the grimacing lady looked at Guru pathetically in the manner of one begging for pity. Her searing pain gored him deep inside. He instantly decided what he had to do, took her in his arms and kissed her goodbye. They then looked into each other's eyes. Finally he said, 'Okay, my life. Close your eyes.'

As she closed her eyes, he took out his kirpan and gave her a resolute stab making sure that she did not dangle long between life and death any further. Her mouth pouted and eyes popped open with the blow. Still, she managed to lung forward in a breathless state to fall in the lap of Guru. He held her tightly for a long while and then checked whether she was still breathing. He could notice no indications of life in her. Also, there were now fewer signs of pain on her face and those too were intermixed with a faint smile. This was the last of her that was going to stick in his mind for ever.

He calmly laid her body on the bed and rang up the local police station to inform that he had killed his wife and they should take him in custody. He also conveyed the information about his location and the landmarks around for the police to reach the place conveniently. His report caused a flurry of activity at the police station. The SHO checked up with the beat constable of the area, if he knew anything about the caller. He was informed that he was a British citizen of Indian origin who had brought his wife suffering from cancer for treatment in the PGI at Chandigarh. The SHO decided to visit the scene of crime himself.

The police party on the spot saw a lifeless female body, bathed in blood, held in the lap of an equally listless man sitting on the blood-stained bed. The neighbours collected at the place identified them as Gursevak Singh and Sukhvinder Kaur. They also disclosed that the man seemed to be deeply devoted to his ailing wife and taking all pains to see that she suffered the least agony while she was alive. They did not have any idea why they ended this way. However, Guru stated to the SHO that he had killed his wife and also pointed to the blood-stained kirpan lying on the floor. The body was removed for post-mortem after being photographed from various angles and after the formality of panchnama (i.e. inquest). The items connected with the crime—blood samples, kirpan, bed sheet, etc. were carefully collected. While examining the scene, the note written by Sukhi was also discovered from under the pillow.

Until now Guru was being treated as a common criminal and ordered to be taken into custody. As a constable reached him with handcuffs, the SHO stopped him. He announced that the lady had written that she was going to kill herself. Guru, however, vehemently insisted that he had stabbed her. The mellowed-down police officer ordered that there was no need to handcuff Guru, as he had submitted to custody. He should just be moved to the police station. Further investigations in the PGI and the fingerprint report established that the case was in the nature of euthanasia. Though under the law it amounted to murder, it was deserving of humane handling. The next day, he was produced before the court where the prosecution did not insist on his police custody. The Sessions Judge was sympathetic too, as the story about this curious case of euthanasia had made prominent headlines in the press and raised a debate whether euthanasia should be decriminalized in certain situations with proper safeguards. The judge committed Guru to judicial custody for fourteen days and passed orders that he would be provided facilities to attend Sukhi's funeral.

Guru had moved to Mohali with Sukhi without informing his relations in India, as he did not want them to crowd around when they were in no position to help them in any manner. He wanted to be alone with Sukhi in the final days of her life. Now that somebody had to make arrangements for her last rites, messages went to Golu and other relations about the incident and the funeral. Some of them had learnt about the incident from the papers and were aghast over her getting into such an agonizing state that she had to beg her loving husband to kill her. They were full of sympathy for the luckless Guru also. They were unable to reconcile with the fact that Guru was a criminal under law. Offers were made to Guru to engage lawyers for him. However, he plainly declined and requested them to disperse after the funeral. He spent generously on her last rites to ensure that his beloved got a decent send off from the world. Golu and Sapna participated in the funeral ceremony apparently in all solemnity and were seen shedding some tears also. However, they were also finding it difficult to suppress their feeling that their father was spending too much money on the ceremonies out of their inheritance which they could have put to better use.

The case was charge-sheeted by the police without delay, as it involved no complications. Their report clearly indicated that it was a case of illegal euthanasia. However, in law, it was culpable homicide amounting to murder. The case also left the conscience-pricked judge in some quandary. Guru had pleaded guilty to the charge of murder against him under Section 302 of the Indian Penal Code and the forensic report and circumstantial evidence clearly supported his plea. Then, his confession itself had been recorded after he had been out of police custody for sufficient time to negate the possibility of any police pressure behind it. So there was no scope in law and on facts of the case not to convict him.

Nonetheless, the humane judge consulted the prosecutor and other eminent lawyers, if the case could be brought in the ambit of section 304 IPC relating to cases of culpable homicide not amounting to murder. But all said, the killing was wilful and it had to be treated as murder under the law. He thus had to convict Guru of murder and asked him, 'What punishment do you think you deserve?'

Guru instantly replied, 'Your honour, I beg for death, as I

want to join my Sukhi in the world next at the earliest.'

The judge smiled and said, 'For that you shall have to wait.'

He sentenced him to life imprisonment, but granted him the status of a 'Better Class Prisoner', even without his pleading for it on the ground that besides being a graduate and an income tax payer, he deserved it on the facts and circumstances of the case too. Simultaneously, he moved his case to the High Court, strongly recommending that it be taken up with the state Home Secretary for clemency at the level of the Governor of the state. All this brought in view that after all, police and judiciary of the country were also human. While doing their duty by the law, they had not failed to express what they felt inside. This also brought in focus the wisdom of the founding fathers of the Indian Constitution in providing for clemency in deserving cases at the top executive levels.

The British, in the normal course, did not follow the policy of keeping convicts in jail at the cost of their revenues. Hangings and floggings, instead, were then the preferred punishments. However, Guru, in view of the peculiar circumstances of his case, would have perhaps been spared the noose even by them.

Golu and Sapna stayed in India till the court proceedings were finalized. From now onwards, it was going to be a long haul for Guru. Moreover, he had lost all will to live. He could hope to be released in seven to eight years in certain circumstances. But he did not think that he would be able to survive even this much. It was, therefore, more or less curtains for him. So, he persuaded Golu to leave for England and move on with his life.

Golu, though sad over what had happened, thought that his father's house would now virtually be his. But this was not to be. Guru's case had evoked wide sympathy in the media. It was, therefore, processed quite promptly in the Home department and moved to the Governor with the state Cabinet approval for granting outright pardon to Guru. His Excellency, the Governor, was also pleased to pass orders granting pardon to him without taking much time. Guru was thus able to return to England in around six months' time.

❦

When he returned home where he had spent some good years of his life with Sukhi, it now looked to be a different place. The master bedroom that they slept in had been occupied by Golu and Sapna. That was alright. After all, life flows in a continuous stream. After them, they were the rightful inheritors of all that their parents possessed. What irked him was that they had already got rid of their very presence in the room. Their portrait in the bloom of their youth and even the one where they were holding baby Golu in their arms stood replaced. Most of the other things dear to them, especially the bonsai plants, had also been removed. On his arrival, they offered to vacate the place, but Guru decided to settle in the guest room. Golu occasionally sat with him and talked nicely, as a son should. However, Guru somehow always wondered, if the family was really happy over his return amongst them.

As time passed, he started getting an impression that the inmates thought of him as the killer of his wife, though they displayed scant regard for her when she was around. The things came to a head when he happened to overhear one day his grandchildren complaining to Sapna that he was a distraction in their studies and she helplessly told them, 'Dears, I do not really know what to do with the old hag.' With that Guru felt that sun had finally set on his family life. He decided there and then that he would not stay with them any longer.

However, asking them straight away to vacate his house would have created an unnecessary turbulence. He instead got them together and suggested that they had not had a family vacation for a long while and they should go for around a fortnight to Spain. They looked confused for a while. But what made the real difference in their mood was the offer of £10,000 by Guru to finance their trip. They quickly arranged for leaves from their employers. The children were already on their vacation. While booking for the tour they took the risk of asking Guru to come along with them. However, to their great relief, the old man opted out.

He saw them off at the Heathrow Airport and then got busy with estate agents to sell his house. His requirement, as posed to them, was to settle the bargain within ten days and he did not mind receiving a little less in price. Since it was a sort of distress sale, they were able to locate a customer post haste. The agreement was drawn on the lines that the purchaser would make the payment within ten days and take possession of the property simultaneously, but allow Guru to keep his household stuff in the service room in their backyard for a month. After that, he would be at liberty to dispose it off the way he liked, if it was not removed by then.

Guru collected the proceeds in his bank account and shifted to a hotel for a while with some personal effects along with some items related to his memories with Sukhi. Upon return from their tour, Golu and his family found the house occupied by the purchaser. After creating some meaningless fuss, they quietly moved to a budget hotel in the vicinity. Golu did not know how his father, who had been bending to his demands all through, could suddenly turn his back on them. They were able to locate him in his hotel room and tried to remonstrate over what he had done to them, though in their heart of hearts they knew that they deserved it. Guru listened to them patiently. That gave them the feeling that they had been able to make suitable impression on him and he would do something to mitigate their problem in the form of some financial help to resettle. They looked hopefully at his expressionless face to finally hear, 'Get lost.' His bluntness just stunned them and they meekly returned without saying a word further.

Now they were left with no option but to come to terms with the difficult situation. It took them a few days to locate a much smaller house on rent and set up their home there. Life was never to be the same for them from now onwards. All extravagance was sucked out from their system. Payment of rent was a great financial drag on them. They started thinking in terms of cutting down on their expenses and laying back something to be able purchase a small house on mortgage basis as early as possible.

❧

After spending a few days in the hotel, Guru shifted to an old-age home, suggestively named 'The Evening'. It was run by a philanthropic trust on no-profit-no-loss basis. Still it was not all that inexpensive. All the inmates here, in some measure or the other, felt abandoned by the world and some of them were in much worse plight than him. He thus ended up feeling, 'Nanak, dukhiya sab sansar.' (O' Nanak, you are not alone in your sadness. All in the world are equally unhappy.) There were a number of occupants in the home from Punjab too. Though Guru now had not been left with anything to live for, he was an optimist by nature. If God wanted him to live for some more time, why not make this time count for something? What is the virtue or wisdom involved in feeling forlorn and appearing, as if you are on a death row here? So, he soon worked towards establishing oneness with the inmates by sharing their joys and sorrows.

Some of the residents here were equally positive in their outlook. So what if their near and dear ones had washed their hands off them, they had built new relationships here. They had time on hand now to do anything they liked and discuss everything under the sun. Those who were able to detach their mind from their past, in fact, felt more comfortable living here. They merrily whiled away their hours in playing cards and other games, watching TV shows and listening to religious discourses or discussing politics. They ate, drank and slept in peace. Occasionally, however, when somebody brought in some family issues in the discussion, all became intent listeners and a cross-thread of sadness then appeared to be running through them all.

There were three old couples in the Home who had shifted here just for convenience because they had no close relations for company. They obviously had no complaints against the world. They were often seen walking around the Home hand in hand. The Home complex was located over a sprawling area in quite some serene surroundings away from the hustle and bustle of the city. However, a regular bus service was available for the occupants to take them to the city, if they had to do some shopping or just felt like being still in the world. The multi-storeyed Home had 120 rooms with attached toilets, along with the necessary infrastructure. It could accommodate around two hundred paying guests and was, indeed, well managed. The management insisted on very little discipline. The occupants could drink at the bar or in their rooms. They could dine in the dining hall or ask for food in their rooms. However, dining hours for various meals were strictly enforced and so were the other little laws. Feedback from the inmates was regularly collected to reshape the welfare measures in line with their needs.

Some inmates were in real bad shape physically, mentally and money-wise too. It was a regular practice for the management of the Home to issue notices to the relations of those who were not able to pay for their expenses. Generally, in such cases, someone or the other always dropped in to clear their dues and assure that they would be more regular in paying for their stay in future. It was clear that their near relations preferred to pay for their stay here, rather than suffer the hassles of taking them home.

Elementary medical facilities were available in the Home itself. Arrangements were also in place to evacuate the seriously ill to the hospitals. However, since it was the gathering of people in the evening of their life, around half a dozen of the occupants kept on departing from the world every year. People here took these sad partings with philosophical stoicism, as these were regular occurrences here. When some kin came to look up their folks here, groups of inmates gathered around them to share their solace. The visitors often brought some delicacies like cakes, fruits, biryani and other dishes loved by their kin. These were often shared among the gathering of friends on the spot. Such gestures were taken to be suggestive of some sort of a bond still subsisting between them and the world. So these infused a bit of cheer in the understandably gloomy ethos of the Home.

The Evening had a nice garden within its complex where the inmates spent most of their day, snacking, drinking and discussing the problems of life and the world when the weather was sunny. There was a kitchen garden also in its backyard. When the management learnt about Gursevak's experience in running a nursery, they approached him to take over the management of the garden and even offered to pay him for it. Guru accepted the responsibility, but declined to accept any payment for it. This assignment provided him a sort of new purpose in life. With inputs in the form of his efforts and expertise, the garden enlivened up further and newer breeds of flowers were seen blooming everywhere. The impact of his involvement was felt in the kitchen garden also. He even initiated action for raising bonsais. All this not only brought him appreciation and applause from the management and the inmates, but also gave him a strange sense of solace and comfort. He saw Sukhi peeping in each flower and often felt that she was working by her side.

Sunil and Varun came to see him often and, occasionally, Prema also accompanied them. They invariably brought some Punjabi dishes like sarson ka saag, gaajar ka halwa, karhi, etc. for Guru to relish and these were always in good quantity for him to be able to share with his friends too. They would sit together reminiscing the happier days of their lives and recounting what they were doing presently. Guru always looked forward to their visits. Their presence made him feel that there was still something well about the world. Sometimes he thought that he would carry some nice memories from the place to Sukhi in the next world and she would feel good about these.

There were a few knowledgeable scholars of Hindu and Sikh scriptures among the occupants of The Evening. They liked to give discourses to the interested guests there. Once a topic cropped up that everything in life revolved round Self. A verse from the Upanishad was quoted to explain this phenomenon. It said that a husband loved his wife and a father his son, not for their sake, but for the reason of their own happiness. Even when a man made sacrifices, he did so because doing so gave him a feeling of comfort. So, everybody should try to stay self-reliant as far as possible and should not view his children as a sort of insurance policy for old age.

This simple observation about the natural pattern of life set many minds thinking. It looked to be of special relevance to the inmates of the The Evening. They were mostly those in whose cases the insurance policy had failed to come good. Guru was also one of them. He, however, had taken care to become self-reliant in good time.

Joining the discussion at this stage, one of the inmates opined, 'That is how communism finally failed, as it happens to be against the grain of nature. It talks of "one for all and all for one", whereas everyone was for himself only. Self was thus the truth.'

The discussion then veered around communism and those not interested in politics started leaving the place.

Years went by. The bonsais raised by Guru were now everywhere in the complex. He felt that his end was also not very far off. Periodically, especially whenever he was unwell, a feeling would creep over his mind, 'Why could Golu not come to see him?' Much that he tried to throw out such thoughts, the sadness on this count kept coming back on him every now and then.

Then, one fine morning, Golu was right before him fighting tears.

Before he could decide how to react, Golu fell in his lap and said among sobs, 'Daddy, we miss you. Please, come back to us.'

'My child, I did try to throw you out from my life, but I could not. Tell me what you want me to do for you now?' Guru managed to say.

'Nothing more now, Dad. You have already done enough for us. I am simply sorry that I could not be worthy of being your son. I even failed to be by the bed of my Mummy when she was dying and needed me most.'

'Sapna and the kids. How are they?'

'They are waiting outside, Dad. They do not know how to face you.'

'They do not have to feel shy of me. Just bring them in,

my child.'

Sapna and the kids were soon before him. Guru threw an affectionate look at them and placed his hand on Sapna's head to bless her. When he took his grandchildren in his arms, they also showed no tendency to squirm out from his embrace, as they used to do. Now, they appeared to be a part of him.

His magnanimity towards them emboldened Sapna to again request him to return to them. She even informed him that they had been able to purchase the same small house where he and Mummy had started their innings in England.

'Daddy, you will feel good there', she suggested.

'Well, my children. I feel the presence of your Mummy while looking after the garden here. I also think that, besides the plants, many of my friends here need me by their side. However, give me a word that you will dispose of my ashes at the same place in India where you immersed your Mummy's. Just a minute, I shall not put any financial burden on you for this.'

He went in his room, wrote a cheque for £10,000 and handed it to Golu.

'Do not shame us further, Dad. We shall do what you want us to do', said Golu with tears rolling over his cheeks and disappearing in his beard. With that, he tore the cheque instantaneously. Guru looked at Sapna to see if there was a twinkle in her glance suggesting that she was unhappy over her husband not accepting the largesse. There was no such flicker to be seen in her eyes. So, the change of heart on their part was real. Perhaps, the absence of any worthwhile struggle in life had spoiled them and the sudden exposure to it had done the trick. Anyway, Guru felt as if lot of load had got removed from his heart and it could beat normally again.

'Okay, my dears. Keep coming as often as you can make it. I shall feel good whenever you are able to show up. My blessings would always be with you.'

They withdrew from the place with some sadness in their heart for being unable to bring their father home. They, however, felt lighter inside that they were at least taking back his blessings and affection with them. The return of his children to him set him thinking afresh. The generational traffic was really a one-way journey or he had just over-reacted to the goings-on in his family. Guru spent that night with his children hovering all around him in his dreams.

❧

Long back, Guru had concluded in his mind that bearing and bringing up children was no guarantee of comfort in old age. People should build up a cushion for the final phase of their life in some other way. The West seemed to have already understood that procreation did not create any value of this sort. In fact, the social systems in developed countries already stood remodelled to help their people in the sunset of their lives. On their part, the citizens should also take timely steps to build adequate corpus for themselves for their future in their productive life.

The sudden change in his situation kept Guru in a contemplative mood for days. Now, what to make out of it? He was clear in his mind that old people with sagging skin and wrinkled faces could not hope to be loved the way they loved their babies. It was also true that some children were nice enough to take their commitment of looking after their aged parents as their sacred duty. He was lucky enough that his children had also at long last joined the ranks of the likes of Sunil and Varun. All said, however, it was equally true that human memory was short and the progeny was unable to recall what all sacrifices were put in by their parents and what all inconveniences were undergone by them to make them stand on their feet in life. The universal truth was that life could be seen as a series of concentric circles. The innermost circle would, of course, be occupied by the Self. The second one would generally be the preserve of one's spouse—as husband and wife are the *Present* of each other. The one after that would go to one's children who are thought of as one's *Future*. The parents, as one's *Past*, who have to be essentially carried along as a burden out of duty, could only hope to be in the fourth circle. All the rest have to be content with the slots further next.

The one-way generational traffic was thus a fact of life. Old age would be easy on nerves, if this simple truth was grasped in time. All would, therefore, do well to organize themselves for the final lap of life in line with this reality.

Acknowledgement

The story has evolved a lot from my discussions on the migrants in the UK that I had with my son-in-law, Bijoy Premi, during our long walks both in India and England.